Main Dish Salads

Main Dish Salads

NORMAN KOLPAS

Photographs by

MICHAEL GRAND

Reader's Digest

The Reader's Digest Association, Inc.
Pleasantville, New York / Montreal

A READER'S DIGEST BOOK

Prepared and produced by
Michael Friedman Publishing Group, Inc.

Editor: Nathaniel Marunas
Designer: Andrea Karman
Design Layout: Lynne Yeamans
Photography Editor: Christopher C. Bain
Production Director: Karen Matsu-Greenberg
Prop sourcing and styling: Leslie Defrancesco
Food preparation and styling: Jennifer Udel

Library of Congress Cataloging-in-Publication Data.

Kolpas, Norman.
    Main dish salads / Norman Kolpas ; photography by Michael Grand.
        p. cm.
    Includes index.
    ISBN 0-7621-0000-1
    1. Salads. 2. Entrées (Cookery)   I. Title
TX740.K665   1998
    641.8'3—dc21   97-38728

Printed and bound in Great Britain by
Butler & Tanner Ltd, Frome and London

Introduction

Oh herbaceous treat!
'Twould tempt the dying anchorite to eat;
Back to the world he'd turn his fleeting soul,
And plunge his fingers in the salad bowl;
Serenely full, the epicure would say
"Fate cannot harm me—I have dined today."

—Sydney Smith, "Recipe for Salad" (1843)

Never have the lines penned by the nineteenth-century English essayist Sydney Smith seemed more prophetic. A glance at any good restaurant's menu today will tell you that we live in an era when the salad has truly come of age, having been elevated to the status of fine dining experience.

This book celebrates main-dish salads in all their diversity. It begins with an overview of the elements that go into making such salads, from a glossary of salad leaves to all the various items that might top them or be tossed with them, including instructions for roasting peppers, peeling and seeding tomatoes, toasting nuts, and making croutons and other crisp bread accompaniments. Following these basics comes an overview of the various elements that make up salad dressings, including recipes for some classic mixtures. These fundamentals are followed by 60 main-dish salad recipes, photographed expressly for this book by Michael Grand and divided into themes: Classics and Variations, Chopped Salads, Robust Salads, and Light and Refreshing Salads. The book concludes with a guide to salad-making equipment and to mail-order ingredients sources.

It is my sincerest hope that you will like the recipes so much that they become standards in your home repertoire, that they will introduce you to a new way of eating meals that are healthy and that refresh and revive your body and spirit even as they satisfy.

—*Norman Kolpas*

Equipment

Most salads are very easy to make and require little if any special equipment. There are, however, a few basic kitchen tools used in making salads, an understanding of which will help you achieve even better results.

Your Hands

I can still remember my astonishment when, as a London-based writer assigned in the mid-1970s to the legendary cooking series *The Good Cook*, I first witnessed renowned cook and series consultant Richard Olney plunge his bare hands deep into a bowl to toss a salad. The gesture seemed downright pagan, a far cry from the fastidious cooking habits of my mother. I loved it.

Olney taught all of us on the series that the best kitchen tools you have are your own hands. Nothing else works as well for letting you judge textures, temperatures, and the degree to which things are blended.

While I wouldn't dream of suggesting that anyone using this book present a beautiful salad to guests at the table and then bury their hands deep within it, do give it a try when you're hidden away in the kitchen. Nor should you forget how useful your hands are for tearing salad greens into bite-size chunks, an essential task that yields results a knife cannot match.

When working with these least-expensive, most invaluable kitchen tools, don't worry that they're somehow unhygienic: Well-washed hands are at least as clean as well-washed mixing spoons. Once you get over any residual squeamishness, you might just discover a new form of fun.

Knives

Good kitchen knives are essential for slicing salad vegetables, carving meat and poultry toppings, and a wide range of other tasks. Yet I am constantly surprised by how *so* many people who aspire to become good cooks try to make do with less-than-good, less-than-sharp knives.

You should seek out a basic set of good-quality knives with sharp, sturdy stainless steel blades and with handles that are securely attached and that feel perfectly comfortable in your hand. For salads, you'll need at the very least a small paring knife, for cutting up small items, for peeling and—yes—paring, and for small, detail-oriented tasks like cutting the cores out of tomatoes; and a so-called chef's knife, which is a medium-size slicing and chopping blade about 8 inches long. I'm also fond of my long, serrated bread/carving knife, which is useful for slicing steak or chicken breast toppings, although you could also use a good, sharp chef's knife for the task.

On the topic of sharpness, another sobering piece of advice needs to be added. Yes, you must be careful around sharp knives, and store them safely in a place—most likely, a wooden knife block—that not only protects their sharp edges but also protects you, your family, and any guests in your kitchen. But you *must* keep those knives sharp. Most home knife-sharpening tools, I find, don't do the trick. We periodically have ours professionally sharpened, either at a knife shop or at a local butcher shop. Remember, too, that a dull knife is far more dangerous than a sharp knife, as it is more likely to slip during cutting.

Cutting Boards

A good kitchen knife is good for nothing without a proper cutting surface. The best choices for cutting boards boil down to two: traditional wooden boards or blocks and acrylic cutting boards.

In my own kitchen, I use the latter type. Most kitchen stores stock several different makes. Look for those that have some give or texture to them, rather than being hard and slick, so that both the knife and the food you are cutting will be less likely to slip.

I keep reading conflicting studies on whether wood or acrylic is supposed to be more hygienic—that is, less likely to harbor bacteria from the foods you prepare. I've even seen some acrylic boards that have bactericidal substances embedded in them. My own practice is, when preparing a recipe that contains both meat (or poultry or seafood) and vegetables requiring cutting, to use one board exclusively for the vegetables and the other exclusively for the raw meat; to further avoid cross-contamination, I tend to use separate knives with each cutting board. Needless to say, good scrubbing with lots of hot water and kitchen soap goes a long way toward maintaining good kitchen hygiene.

Other Cutting Tools

A wide variety of other kitchen cutting tools can be useful when preparing salads. Among them are vegetable peelers, of which I find the swivel-bladed variety the most efficient; citrus zesters, small tools with sharp-edged holes that remove citrus zest in thin little strips; and, most important, a handheld box grater/shredder, which you can use to quickly grate citrus zest or a hard cheese like Parmesan, or shred anything from a carrot to a block of Cheddar cheese.

Grill Pans

A number of the recipes in this book call for the featured topping for a salad to be broiled or grilled. I want here to offer one more option, the grill pan, which is becoming increasingly available and which offers both the convenience of broiling and much of the appealing results of outdoor grilling.

Grill pans are a type of stove top cookware, usually made of cast-iron or heavy-gauge aluminum, that have raised parallel ridges across their surface. Often, their surfaces are also treated to be stick-resistant. Heated on top of your stove's burner, they build up an intense heat that can sear-cook steak, chicken breasts, or seafood, cooking them quickly while endowing them with the

kind of char marks you usually only get from an outdoor grill.

You'll find such grill pans, usually imported from Europe, with increasing frequency in well-stocked, high-quality kitchen equipment stores. They are well worth seeking out, and can certainly be used with ease to cook any of the grilled salad toppings on these pages.

Salad Spinners

In my time, I've owned several salad spinners, those devices that hold just-washed salad leaves in a slotted basket that is made to spin by hand-crank or pulley, and thus fling all the water off the leaves into the outer container. Mine always seem to wear out, though—maybe because they're so much fun to play with. (When my son, Jacob, was a toddler, he played with one incessantly until it wouldn't spin anymore.)

By all means get one if you like. In fact, seek out an old-fashioned French salad spinner, a wire basket in which you enclose the leaves and then, grasping the basket by its handle, step out into the yard and spin it round and round at the end of your swinging arm.

Just the same, most salad leaves will dry out just fine if you spread them out on good, absorbent cotton kitchen towels and then loosely roll them up. (See also my suggestions on pages 14–15 for storing and crisping salad leaves in the refrigerator.)

Mixing Bowls

Salad making, it seems to me, demands more mixing bowls than just about any other type of cooking: bowls in which to mix dressings, bowls in which to marinate featured ingredients, bowls to hold separate elements of a salad before you assemble the final presentation, and bowls in which to toss and mix all the ingredients together.

When purchasing your bowls, look for items made of sturdy, heavy glassware, glazed earthenware, or ceramic, none of which is likely to react with acidic ingredients.

When selecting the size bowl you'll need for any task, first estimate all the measured-out ingredients that you'll be putting into or combining in the bowl. Then, select a bowl of a size that looks like it will comfortably hold those ingredients. Finally, put that bowl aside and pick the next largest size. That's my own time-tested strategy for ensuring that you'll always have enough room to mix things properly.

This brings me to the topic of large salad bowls. Many of the salads in this book call for as much as sixteen cups of salad leaves alone to serve four people. That quantity translates to a one-gallon-capacity bowl, and, allowing for other ingredients and room to toss things thoroughly, it really demands a two-gallon bowl—or, that you prepare the salad in separate batches.

Most nesting bowl sets don't come with that large a bowl, so you'll have to buy a big salad bowl as well. A good place to look for inexpensive ones, I've found, is at a professional restaurant supply store, where you'll find giant, hemispherical bowls made of plastic, aluminum, or stainless steel—perfectly utilitarian tools that you can use to mix up a giant mess of salad.

Salad Servers

If I remember correctly after all these years, my wife and I got among our wedding presents at least three different sets of salad servers—you know, those long, giant fork-and-spoon pairs that folks insist you need to toss and serve a salad. Whenever I can tactfully do so, I avoid using them (see my previous comments on hands as kitchen tools). However, I still do occasionally break them out when the need arises to toss and serve a salad at the table.

I can't make any recommendation about design. There are so many different "salad sets"—big salad bowls, serving bowls and servers, all wrapped up together as a gift. They're all very stylish, so choosing a design is really a matter of taste. I do have stronger feelings, though, about material. Smooth plastic, acrylic, or metal servers, I find, are too slippery, easily losing their grip on salad leaves that have been slicked with dressing. Wood, for me, is a much better choice of material, having enough of a textured surface to really grasp the ingredients of a salad, no matter how slippery, and thus making tossing easier.

Serving Plates and Bowls

Main dish salads call for big, dinner-size plates or bowls rather than the more demure containers normally used for salads. At a minimum, the salads in this book require plates about 10 inches in diameter and, for those with a lot of leaves and other ingredients, deep bowls of about the same width. I also find myself frequently serving salads in Italian-style pasta bowls, wide, shallow containers about 2 to 3 inches deep.

The most important piece of advice I can give you on choosing your serving plates and bowls, though, is to use your imagination. Just as most of the recipes in this book break the conventional boundaries of the salad world, so too should you feel absolutely free to break from convention and serve your creations in whatever containers are at hand, work sufficiently well for the given recipe, and help make your presentation as attractive as possible.

A Guide to Salad Ingredients

Although relatively easy to prepare, main-dish salads are, by their very nature, more complex constructions than their familiar appetizer or side-dish cousins. Each element of a main-dish salad plays a particular role, its tastes, textures, shapes, and colors dynamically interplaying with the other parts of the salad. The following guide should give you a good idea of how this give-and-take among ingredients works, while introducing you to the basic elements of the main dish salad.

Salad Leaves

The leaves you use—and I say "leaves" rather than the more popular words "greens" or "lettuces" to reflect the wider variety of choices available to cooks today—go a long way toward determining the personality of the salad you make.

Despite the incredible variety of leaves available today to most cooks, you'll notice that in most of the recipes in this book I suggest only *types* of leaves, such as bitter greens, or call for generic blends, such as mixed baby salad leaves. When I make a specific recommendation, it is for leaves that are likely to be available in most markets, such as romaine or butter lettuce; in my Test Kitchen Notes, I suggest other options if you are unable to find the kinds of leaves mentioned in the ingredients list.

BELGIAN ENDIVE

Small, slender, cylindrical heads of crisp-but-tender, spear-shaped leaves prized for their refreshing, slightly bitter taste. Smaller, paler-colored heads, tending toward white and yellow-green rather than darker shades of green, have a subtler, more pleasant flavor. Good with fairly strong-tasting toppings or mixed with other leaves.

CHARD

(also called Swiss Chard)

Chard has vibrant, green leaves and broad white or red stems. Leaves should be springy to the touch, stems in a compact bunch, the bases connected to each other at the bottom. Slightly bitter in flavor, this vitamin-rich green can be used like spinach in combination with other leaves or with strong-tasting ingredients.

ARUGULA

(also called Rocket, Rugula, and Roquette)

Fairly strong-tasting, pleasantly bitter and slightly peppery leaves, resembling spinach in their deep green color and relatively tender texture. Good on their own as a background for robust ingredients, or mixed with milder leaves.

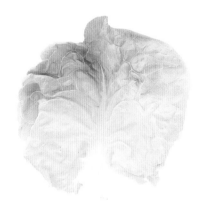

BUTTER LETTUCE

(also called Bibb, Boston, and Limestone)

Very tender, small, frilly leaves with a pale green color and a delicate, mild taste. Best as a background for more subtly flavored ingredients or those with delicate texture.

ICEBERG LETTUCE

A classic, cool, crisp, old-fashioned favorite, with a mild, unassertive flavor. The pale green leaves make attractive "cups" for lining serving plates.

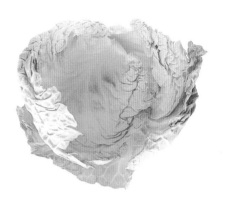

NAPA CABBAGE

Very mild-tasting variety of cabbage with long leaves composed of crisp white ribs and very crinkly leaves. Excellent in Asian-style salads.

RED CABBAGE

(also called Purple Cabbage)

Tightly packed, deep purple leaves with an assertive flavor and crisp texture that may be moderated by shredding and briefly dousing with boiling water. A standby in slaw-type salads.

ROMAINE

Very crisp lettuce whose long, ribbed leaves have a distinctive but not assertive flavor; inner leaves taste milder and have a softer texture.

RADICCHIO

Smallish heads of bright, deep purplish-red leaves with white ribs, a moderately crisp, cabbagelike texture and, particularly in smaller leaves, a pleasant, bracingly bitter taste that complements strong-flavored ingredients. Radicchio is often included in salad leaf mixtures for its color.

RED-LEAF LETTUCE

Tender, fairly large, loose leaves with a mild taste that belies its assertive appearance.

SAVOY CABBAGE

Medium-green cabbage whose leaves have a moderate flavor and a very crinkly appearance that lends itself to attractive presentations.

SPINACH

Pleasantly earthy-tasting, tender leaves that lend themselves very well to robust-flavored salads. Larger leaves can tend toward a tougher texture and stronger flavor, as well as having stringy ribs, and they require tearing into bite-size pieces. Baby spinach leaves are prized for their milder taste, tenderness, and highly attractive appearance.

WATERCRESS

Peppery-tasting, refreshingly cool and crisp sprigs of dark green little leaves that nicely complement rich or strong-tasting ingredients.

Mixed Baby Salad Leaves

Immature forms of many of the leaves mentioned above, along with other, more esoteric leaves and herbs, are being widely marketed today as mixed baby salad leaves, sold loose in market stalls or already washed, dried, bagged, and labeled. The culinary advantages of such mixtures lie in their freshness of flavor, their tenderness, the variety of subtle tastes and textures they present, and the beautiful presentations they offer. For the busy cook, they also offer the advantage of ease—just fill a bag, or grab an already filled one, and you have the foundation of a main-dish salad right in your hand.

With such quality and ease in mind, many of the recipes in this book call for such leaves. However, if the markets you frequent do not offer them, buy instead the smallest, tenderest specimens of whatever variety of salad leaves are available to you, even if that amounts to only one or two types. And if you can't get true baby leaves, simply buy the smallest heads on display and select the smaller, inner leaves; or tear larger leaves into bite-size pieces.

Again, use such mixtures if they are convenient for you. If they aren't, never let their lack of availability keep you from enjoying any main-dish salad in this book.

Selecting and Preparing Salad Leaves

Vegetables of all kinds, including salad leaves, are fresher, cleaner, and more ready to be eaten today than they ever were in the past. That doesn't mean, however, that you should skimp on the attention you pay to readying the leaves you buy for the table.

When shopping for salad leaves, seek out those that are bright and fresh-looking, well-formed, and free of blemishes. Don't get hung up on dirt, which can be washed off at home; look past it to the quality of the leaves themselves. Avoid anything that appears to be drooping or has any brown spots. When selecting prepackaged leaves, check to see if there is a use-by date, then look through the clear parts on the wrapper, applying the same criteria as above and paying special attention to detect any rotting leaves.

Once at home, store leaves in the crisper drawer of your refrigerator and use within a day or two if you can; of course, the leaves will last longer, but they will diminish in texture and flavor.

Don't wash leaves until shortly before use, because any water left clinging to them for too long can hasten their decline. Except for very hard, tightly packed cabbages and the like, separate leaves by hand rather than with a knife, to avoid damaging or bruising them.

Rinse off any dirt under cold running water, except in the case of spinach, which grows in very sandy soil and is prone to hold on to its dirt. For spinach, fill a sink or basin with cold water, then immerse the leaves in it and slosh them around. Next, lift the leaves out of the water and set them aside, then drain the sink or basin and rinse out the sand that will have settled on the bottom. Repeat the procedure until the spinach leaves no residue of sand when lifted out.

After leaves are washed, dry them in a salad spinner (see page 8) or by patting them between clean kitchen towels or double thicknesses of paper toweling. Then gently roll up the leaves in the towels to hold in the refrigerator until the time comes to assemble the salad.

Do not cut or tear leaves until just before serving time. Cutting is necessary for hardy leaves like those of cabbage, or when particularly fine-textured effects are desired, as for slaws or chopped salads. In all other cases, simply tear the salad leaves into bite-size pieces with your fingers. The results will be more pleasingly varied than uniformly cut leaves, and they will be less subject to unsightly bruising and discoloration.

Other Vegetables

A cornucopia of other vegetables make appearances in main-dish salads. The following entries highlight some of the more common choices. Particulars on more unusual or less frequently used ingredients may be found in the Test Kitchen Notes of individual recipes in which they appear.

THE ONION FAMILY

Various kinds of onions and their cousins give sharp, biting flavor and crisp, crunchy texture to main-dish salads. Most often, they are used to highlight other ingredients rather than call attention to themselves. For that reason, I tend to shy away from using garlic in main-dish salads, with the exception of its indispensability in various kinds of Caesar salad (see pages 30–36). When I want a fairly pungent effect, I opt instead for shallots, whose flavor tends to hover midway between that of garlic and onion. My favorite kind of salad onions are sweet varieties that, though offering good onion flavor, also possess a distinctive overlay of sugary mildness, with none of the harshness of other onions. Sweet brown-skinned varieties include those grown near and named after Maui, Hawaii; Walla Walla, Washington; and Vidalia, Georgia. Sweet Texas varieties also exist. If you can't find these, red onions are a good alternative.

BELL PEPPERS

The mild, vaguely bell-shaped members of the pepper family, known as bell peppers, have an important role in salads both in their raw form and roasted (see recipe below). Raw peppers have a wonderfully juicy crispness and a nice, sharp bite of flavor that grows mellower and sweeter as the peppers ripen from their green state to various shades of red (the most common ripened form), yellow, and orange. These different, bright hues also lend attractive color to salads. To prepare raw bell peppers for salads, their tough stems and indigestible seeds and spongy white internal ribs must first be removed. Use a sharp knife to cut a pepper in halves or quarters vertically through the stem and flower end; then, with your fingers, pull out the stem sections and the clusters of seeds attached to it, as well as any remaining seeds and ribs inside each piece. Cut up the stemmed and seeded peppers as called for in the recipe. (Note that the same technique applies to preparing raw chili peppers for salads. Bear in mind, however, that you must exercise great caution when handling hot chilies, as their volatile oils can burn your skin, any cuts or abrasions, or your eyes. If your hands are particularly sensitive, wear rubber gloves when preparing chilies. Wash your hands with lots of warm, soapy water, and do not touch your eyes or other sensitive areas.)

When roasted until their shiny skins blister and blacken, bell peppers develop a wonderful sweetness and become tender and juicy, making a wonderful embellishment for many main-dish salads. If you are in a rush to use such peppers in a salad, keep on hand jars of roasted peppers, packed in salted water or in oil (often sold in the condiments sections of food stores or in Italian delicatessens). For the absolute best flavor and texture, however, roast the peppers yourself.

To roast peppers, preheat the broiler. Place the peppers on a foil-lined baking sheet or dish beneath the broiler and cook them, turning them occasionally until their skins are evenly blackened and blistered, 10 to 15 minutes. Remove them from the broiler and cover them with another sheet of foil, leaving them at room temperature until they are cool enough to handle. Then, with your fingers, peel off the blistered skins; tear or cut open the peppers, taking special care in case any steam lingers inside them. Remove and discard the stems, ribs, and seeds, using a small spoon if necessary to pick up any errant seeds. As a bonus, save the juices that run from the peppers. They have a sweet flavor that can enhance a salad dressing.

FRESH TOMATOES

Especially in summer, when vine-ripened varieties appear in markets and offer cooks the best in firm, juicy-crisp texture and intensely sweet-savory flavor, tomatoes are a significant part of main-dish salads. Shun, however, most hot-house varieties, which tend to be mushy and flavorless. For the best all-around tomato at any time of year, seek out the small, cylindrical variety known as the Roma tomato, also sometimes sold as Italian or plum tomatoes. Tomatoes should never be refrigerated, as they lose their flavor and texture as a result of the cold; instead, leave unused tomatoes in the open or in a paper bag on the counter so that their delicious flavor and meaty texture are maintained.

The peels and seeds of tomatoes offer nothing to salads, being indigestible and flavorless. However, for the most part there is no need to remove them,

except for the most fastidious of presentations or for those salads whose appearance, taste, or texture might be lessened by the watery matter that surrounds tomato seeds.

To peel tomatoes, bring a saucepan of water to a boil and, on the counter nearby, set a mixing bowl full of ice and water. Use the tip of a small, sharp knife to cut out the cores of the tomatoes, then score a shallow X in the opposite, flower ends. With a slotted spoon, lower the tomatoes into the boiling water for about 20 seconds, immersing them completely to loosen their skins, then transfer them to the ice water to chill. Using your fingers or the knife, peel off the skins. Then cut the tomatoes crosswise in half and, with your fingertips or the handle of a teaspoon, scoop out the seed sacs from each half (of course, you can seed an uncooked tomato in the same fashion).

Pastas

All kinds of pastas can add hearty flavor and chewy texture to salads, whether they embellish a main-dish mixture or replace most of the salad greens in one of the main-dish pasta salads you'll find scattered throughout this book. You'll find specifics on different types of pasta—including Asian noodles—in the Test Kitchen Notes of individual recipes. Take care to cook pasta for salads only until tender but still chewy, what the Italians call *al dente*, "to the tooth." This is because the pasta will soak up some of the dressing and contin-

ue to soften slightly; so *al dente* cooking will ensure perfectly textured, nonmushy pasta in your salad.

Cheeses

For many people, a main-dish salad simply does not qualify unless it includes the richness and, sometimes, the tang of good cheese. You'll find fairly common cheeses such as Cheddar, Swiss, Jack, blue, and Parmesan used in various recipes throughout this book. Less familiar to some will be the fresh, creamy goat cheese I sometimes call for, available in both imported and domestic forms in well-stocked dairy departments and specialty shops.

Red Meat

One of the marvelous things about a main-dish salad is the way it enables you to stretch a little bit of red meat a long way, one of the tenets of the health-conscious contemporary diet. When recipes in this book call for beef steak, lamb, or pork, you'll find that the quantity divides up to no more than about 4 ounces per serving. Yet, you get to enjoy the meat's rich savor, backed up and complemented by a wide variety of vegetables. Because meat stars in some of the most elegant main-dish salads in this book, you will want to seek out the best supplier available for well-trimmed, high-quality meats.

Poultry

Poultry in main-dish salads means white-meat chicken, one of the healthiest choices for protein available today. The recipes in this book take advantage of the widespread availability and convenience of ready-to-cook boneless, skinless chicken breasts. Still other salads in this book utilize leftover chicken, making them ideal choices for lunch or a light dinner on the day after you've roasted a whole bird.

Seafood

Grilled seafood fillets such as salmon or tuna, or freshly grilled shrimp or scallops, are especially pleasurable toppings for light and flavorful main-dish salads. Seek out a fishmonger, whether in a supermarket or a specialty shop or stall, that offers you a good choice of fresh, high-quality seafood, and never buy anything that doesn't look clear, moist, and fresh, and have any aroma about it other than the fresh, clean scent of the sea. A good fishmonger will also have available two of the most convenient items for main-meal seafood salads: freshly cooked lump crabmeat and tiny, sweet, already-cooked baby bay shrimp.

Nuts and Seeds

Nuts of all kinds—including peanuts, almonds, walnuts, pecans, hazelnuts, macadamias, and pine nuts—add crunch and savor to salads, as do toasted sesame seeds. Toasting makes them all the crunchier and richer (and enables you to remove the skins of hazelnuts).

Toasted Nuts and Sesame Seeds

1. Preheat the oven to 325°F.

2. Spread the nuts or sesame seeds in a single layer on a foil-lined baking sheet or baking dish. Bake the nuts just until they are light golden brown, turning them occasionally with a wooden spoon and checking frequently to guard against scorching. Roasting time will depend on size: sesame seeds will need no more than about 1 minute, pine nuts or slivered almonds 3 to 5 minutes, whole nuts up to 10 minutes. The residual heat in the nuts will continue to darken them slightly after removal from the oven.

3. After roasting hazelnuts, fold them inside a kitchen towel and rub vigorously to loosen their skins. After they have cooled, use your fingertips to remove any residual bits of skin, but don't bother to remove any pieces that remain clinging tightly.

Breads

No salad meal is complete without a crusty loaf of bread, ready to complement the food, cleanse the palate between bites, and sop up the last traces of dressing and juices once the salad is gone. I am an avid exponent of the boutique-style, high-quality bakeries that seem to be popping up everywhere—a trend that happily shows no signs of abating. Indeed, in many supermarkets nowadays you'll find special displays featuring the fresh-baked products of local custom bakeries. Seek out your own local ones, and have a field day choosing one or more types of special breads that you feel will best complement the main-dish salads you plan to prepare.

Bread, of course, also plays a more integral role in main-dish salads in the form of croutons, crostini, and toasts. The following recipes offer some classic basics and variations called for in several of the salad recipes in this book. Use a firm-textured, white or sourdough country-style loaf, such as an Italian *filone* or French *flûte* or *baguette*, preferably purchased from a quality bakery. For the best results, the bread should be a day or two old so that its crumb will have firmed up and dried out sufficiently for you to cut it into cubes that will toast up well. If you want to use up a whole loaf, you can double or triple the recipe and store the toasts in an airtight container for several days.

Croutons

4 slices country-style white bread, cut
  ½-inch-thick
6 tablespoons extra-virgin olive oil or
  melted unsalted butter

1. Preheat the oven to 350°F.

2. With a sharp knife, cut the bread slices into ½-inch cubes (trim off the crusts only if you want to). Put the cubes in a mixing bowl and, tossing them continuously but gently, drizzle in the oil or butter to coat them evenly.

3. Spread the cubes in a single layer on a baking sheet and bake, turning them once or twice, until evenly golden brown, about 15 minutes. Let them cool to room temperature, then store in an airtight container until ready to use.

Variations

GARLIC CROUTONS

With a garlic press, squeeze 1 or 2 peeled garlic cloves into a small bowl and stir together with the oil or butter before mixing with the bread cubes.

GARLIC-SPICE CROUTONS

Along with the garlic above, stir in a pinch of pure ground red chili powder or paprika with the oil or butter.

LEMON-GARLIC CROUTONS

Along with the garlic above, stir in 1 tablespoon finely grated lemon zest with the oil or butter.

GARLIC-PARMESAN CROUTONS

Along with the garlic above, stir in 2 tablespoons freshly grated Parmesan cheese with the oil or butter.

FAT-FREE GARLIC CROUTONS

Before cutting the bread slices into cubes, use a garlic press to purée 1 or 2 garlic cloves and spread the garlic all over both sides of each slice.

TEST KITCHEN NOTES

THE CRISPLY TOASTED CUBES OF BREAD KNOWN AS CROUTONS ADD RICH CRUNCH AND SAVOR TO SALADS, AS WELL AS THE SPARK OF WHATEVER SEASONINGS YOU MIGHT ADD TO THE CROUTONS (SEE ACCOMPANYING VARIATIONS). THE ESSENTIAL ELEMENT, OF COURSE, IS GOOD BREAD.

USE YOUR CHOICE OF OLIVE OIL OR BUTTER, OR A BLEND.

Crostini

¾ cup extra-virgin olive oil
2 dozen diagonal ¼-inch-thick slices from
  a long, narrow white bread loaf

1. Preheat the oven to 375°F.

2. Dipping a pastry brush repeatedly into the olive oil, evenly brush both sides of each bread slice with the oil. Place the slices on a foil-lined baking sheet.

3. Bake until the toasts are crisp and golden-brown, about 6 minutes on each side. Serve immediately.

> **TEST KITCHEN NOTES**
>
> THESE ITALIAN-STYLE BREAD TOASTS MAY BE TUCKED INTO THE SIDES OF SALADS OR SERVED IN PLACE OF BREAD.

Parmesan Toasts

¾ cup unsalted butter, softened
1 cup freshly grated Parmesan cheese
2 dozen diagonal ¼-inch-thick slices from
  a long, narrow, white bread loaf

1. Preheat the oven to 375°F.

2. In a shallow bowl, use a fork to mash together the butter and cheese. With a table knife, generously spread the butter-cheese mixture onto one side of each bread slice. Place the slices buttered sides up on a foil-lined baking sheet.

3. Bake until the bread and its topping are crisp and golden-brown, about 12 minutes. Serve immediately.

Variations

GARLIC-PARMESAN TOASTS

With a garlic press, purée 1 or 2 garlic cloves into the mixing bowl, mashing them together with the butter and cheese.

GARLIC TOASTS

Omit the cheese and, with a garlic press, purée 1 or 2 garlic cloves into the mixing bowl, mashing them together with the butter.

> **TEST KITCHEN NOTES**
>
> THESE CRISP, SAVORY TOASTS MAKE A NICE COMPLEMENT TO ROBUST SALADS, PILED ON TOP OF THE BED OF GREENS OR SERVED FROM A NAPKIN-LINED BASKET ON THE SIDE.
>
> YOU CAN VARY THE RECIPE TO YOUR TASTE BY ADDING OTHER SEASONINGS, OR BY LEAVING OUT THE CHEESE (SEE ACCOMPANYING VARIATIONS).

CHAPTER 2

The Art of the Dressing

Dressing is the sauce of a main dish salad. Like any sauce, it contributes unique character through its taste and texture, while marrying all the salad's diverse ingredients by uniformly coating them.

Achieving the delicate balance between the leaves and the dressing is part of the art of dressing a salad. It is important to select the dressing's specific ingredients for their individual properties as well as how they suit your own tastes, a point that applies particularly to flavored oils like olive oil (see pages 23–24). Actually adding the dressing and tossing the salad is the final part of the art.

On the topic of tossing, in the recipes in this book I simply tell you at what point to toss the salad. It is worth stressing here, however, that salads should be adequately dressed to your taste and well tossed. In my testing, I have striven to include ample dressing for each recipe, because I generally like salads that are generously dressed and think that most other people do as well. Because most of the recipes call for the dressing to be mixed and held separately until serving time, however, you have the option of adding only as much dressing as you like, or of passing dressing separately for guests to serve themselves.

As for tossing, there's an old Italian saying that salads should be tossed thirty-three times, once for each year of Jesus' life. Not that there's any deep spiritual connection to the tossing of a salad. I think that was just a vivid way to remind a religious people that salads should be tossed well. Don't shy away from the task. If you're tossing the salad in the kitchen, dare to plunge your (well-washed) hands into the salad bowl so you can turn over all the ingredients and mix them up thoroughly, feeling with your fingertips that precise moment when they are all well and truly coated with the dressing. Be careful not to toss the salad for so long that it bruises and becomes limp, and don't leave the greens in an acidic dressing for too long before serving; if you do, the greens will become disagreeably limp.

Making and Buying Salad Dressings

A majority of the salad recipes in this book include recipes for their own custom dressings, a nod to the fact that a creative salad often has a dressing specifically tailored to its ingredients.

But *please* do not forsake any bottled dressings you might love. I never wish to be called a snob where any food is concerned, and I would hate for you to feel that bottled dressings are unacceptable for the salads in this book.

Vinegars and Other Acidic Ingredients

Vinegars and other acidic ingredients contribute bracing sharpness to a salad.

BALSAMIC VINEGAR

This is the gold standard of vinegars, a specialty of Modena, Italy, made by steeping and reducing fine wine vinegar in a succession of ever-smaller wooden kegs over many years, for up to several decades. It has a deep, tawny red color and incredibly rich taste with an edge of sweetness, and the finest, oldest varieties can have an almost syruplike consistency.

CIDER VINEGAR

Made from apple cider, this vinegar gives that fruit's characteristic tangy sweetness to dressings in which it is included.

FRUIT VINEGARS

These may be made by fermenting a fruit wine or, more commonly, by steep-

ing fresh fruit such as raspberries in wine vinegar. You'll see that, with the exception of one salad in this book, I don't specifically call for fruit vinegars; when I want a fruit-flavored salad, I add fruit to it.

HERB VINEGARS

The same grumpy comment I made in the preceding paragraph also applies to vinegars flavored by steeping fresh herbs in them. While some such products can be nice, and you are certainly free to substitute them for other wine-based vinegars I call for in this book, my own preference is to add fresh or dried herbs to salads or their dressings.

LEMON JUICE AND OTHER CITRUS JUICES

Sharply acidic, slightly sweet lemon juice is a fine substitute for wine vinegar in dressings intended for light salads, particularly those featuring seafood or white-meat chicken. (In a few recipes in this book, I also use orange juice to make a pleasantly sweet and tangy dressing.) Please don't resort to using bottled lemon juice; always squeeze it fresh from whole lemons. You'll note that I usually include a little sugar in the seasonings for lemon-based dressing; this not only counteracts some of its acidity but actually serves to highlight the lemony flavor in the dressing.

RICE VINEGAR

Distilled from rice wine, this light, mild vinegar works well in dressings for Asian-style salads. I prefer to buy a Japanese variety designated as "seasoned" rice vinegar, which includes a little bit of sugar that adds a pleasant sweet edge to dressings in which it is used.

SHERRY VINEGAR

A vinegar fermented from the fortified, cask-aged wine of Jerez, Spain, and notable for the rich, sweet-edged, nut-like taste it shares with that wine.

WINE VINEGARS

Vinegar fermented from red or white wine and sharing all the distinctive properties of the wine from which it is made. For that reason, select good-quality wine vinegars; you may even wish to experiment with vinegars made from specific white or red wine varietals such as Chardonnay or Pinot Noir.

Oils, Mayonnaise, and Other Fats

While the acidic element of a dressing gives it and the salad much of its characteristic flavor and bracing sharpness, the oils or other fats in the dressing serve another, multiple role. First, they act as the medium by which the dressing clings, coating salad leaves and other ingredients. They also contribute richness, in taste, in body, and in the way the dressing feels in the mouth. Finally, many forms of fat contribute their own distinctive flavor to a salad dressing, although some dressings instead make use of flavorless vegetable oils when a less complex flavor effect is desired. Below are some of the most common choices for oils and other salad dressing enrichments, as used in this book.

CREAM AND SOUR CREAM

Both these dairy products sometimes enrich salad dressings. Whipping cream makes a lovely dressing when combined with lemon juice, which serves to thicken it. Sour cream can add a rich note to some mayonnaise-based dressings.

MAYONNAISE

This thick emulsion of oil and egg yolks makes a wondrous enrichment for some old-fashioned salads. I used to make my own mayonnaise for salads. Today, given the widespread health concerns regarding the use of raw egg yolks, it is wiser to use commercial mayonnaise,

and some excellent brands exist. When this book calls for mayonnaise, buy the best quality you can, and steer clear of products labeled "mayonnaise dressing" or "salad dressing" or other names that indicate it isn't pure, real mayonnaise. Note, however, that many manufacturers also now sell reduced-fat mayonnaise, which can be an excellent choice if you are trying to lower your dietary fat intake.

NUT OILS

Some specific dressing recipes may call for oils expressed from flavorful nuts, such as hazelnuts or walnuts, to contribute the rich, deep taste of that particular nut. Be sure to buy good-quality products made from toasted nuts, which will have fuller flavor. You will also see peanut oil in the stores. It has just a hint of that nut's richness, making it a good addition to Asian salads, but it is predominately flavorless and may be used as an all-purpose oil. (Note, however, that many people are severely allergic to peanuts, and that allergy extends to the oil as well.) Nut oils go rancid fairly quickly, so buy the smallest quantity you can and store in an airtight container in a cool place.

OLIVE OIL

The oil expressed from ripe olives has a rich, fruity flavor that makes it the best, most versatile oil for dressing salads. For the recipes in this book, I specify extra-virgin olive oil, the designation for oil extracted on the first pressing without the use of heat or any chemical extractants.

SESAME SEED OIL

This is an oil pressed from sesame seeds, which enriches dressings for Asian-style salads. Do not, however, buy the pale golden sesame oils sold in some health-food stores; seek, instead, Asian-style

sesame oil, which has a deep golden-brown color that results from toasting the seeds before the oil is pressed.

VEGETABLE OILS

This general term refers to oils or oil blends made from corn, canola, or saf-flower seeds, noted for their light, unob-trusive flavors.

Seasonings

Most salad dressing recipes begin with stirring salt and pepper into vinegar until the salt has dissolved, with seasoning a necessary first step because the presence of oil can hamper the dissolving. Salt, as it does in most cases, heightens the flavor of the salad, with the exact amount used determined by the relative saltiness of the other ingredients. In Asian salads, soy sauce often replaces the salt. In lemon-based dressings, a little sugar joins the salt to heighten the fruity flavor. White pepper tends to replace black pepper in more delicately flavored dishes, or in those in which you don't want black specks to mar the appearance.

Still other seasonings go a long way to adding character to dressings. Mustard, in its creamy form, provides the extra benefit of emulsifying the dressing, giving it both body and a uni-form consistency. Among the many other seasonings available, the most common are probably the various forms of fresh herbs—particularly basil, chives, dill, and parsley (preferably the more flavor-ful broad-leafed Italian variety)—that may be found in the produce sections of supermarkets and in farmers' markets.

Although that sounds fairly specific, on a visit to the oils section of virtually any market you'll find an incredible range of extra-virgin olive oils to choose from. They vary in color, in translucency, and in taste depending on the kinds of olives they were pressed from, where they were grown, the equipment that was used, and how the oil was filtered. As a rule, the darker green the color, the stronger its flavor. Select an olive oil for salad dressings that best suits the other salad ingredients as well as your personal tastes; more specifically, whether or not you like the taste of olive oil. Note, too, that extra-virgin olive oils labeled "light" are not light on calories or fat, having just as much of both as any oil, but rather are light in flavor.

Basic Vinaigrette

¼ cup wine or balsamic vinegar
½ teaspoon salt
¼ teaspoon pepper
¾ cup extra-virgin olive oil

In a small mixing bowl, stir together the vinegar, salt, and pepper with a fork or small wire whisk, until the salt dissolves. Stirring continuously, slowly pour in the olive oil. Set the dressing aside.

Variations

LEMON VINAIGRETTE

Substitute lemon juice for the vinegar, adding ½ to ¾ teaspoon sugar along with the salt and pepper.

DIJON MUSTARD VINAIGRETTE

As soon as the salt and pepper have been added, stir in 1 teaspoon of creamy Dijon mustard before adding the oil.

TEST KITCHEN NOTES

Literally a "little vinegar" sauce, this classic, most basic, simple, and versatile salad dressing relies on the quality of the oil and the vinegar you use. While I give basic proportions here, you'll find many variations on it.

Proportions of vinegar to oil can vary from 1 part to 2 parts, 1 to 3, or more, depending again on the individual properties of your ingredients and the salad you are dressing. Use the accompanying recipe as a starting point for your own experiments.

Classic Blue Cheese Dressing

½ cup mayonnaise
½ cup sour cream
¾ cup crumbled blue cheese
Black pepper

In a mixing bowl, stir together the mayonnaise, sour cream, and blue cheese until evenly blended. Season to taste with black pepper, stirring it in thoroughly. Cover the bowl with plastic wrap and refrigerate until serving time.

TEST KITCHEN NOTES

I find that both mayonnaise and sour cream are essential to get the right balance of creaminess and rich tang to back up the flavor of the cheese.

You might also try crumbling the cheese into a basic vinaigrette, especially one made with balsamic vinegar. The resulting Italian-style blue cheese dressing can be spectacular on meaty salads, especially those featuring steak.

If you freshly grind the pepper, set your grinder to a coarse setting and the dressing will give you occasional little pungent bites of pepper flavor. Don't add salt: you'll get enough from the cheese and from any common brand of mayonnaise.

Ranch Dressing

MAKES ABOUT 1½ CUPS

¾ cup buttermilk
¾ cup mayonnaise
1 teaspoon lemon juice
¼ small onion, grated
1 teaspoon finely chopped fresh chives
        or ½ teaspoon dried chives
1 teaspoon finely snipped fresh dill or
        ½ teaspoon dill weed
1 teaspoon finely chopped Italian parsley
½ to ¾ teaspoon salt

In a mixing bowl, stir together the buttermilk, mayonnaise, and lemon juice until smoothly blended. Add the onion and herbs and stir them in. Season to taste with salt. Cover the bowl with plastic wrap and refrigerate until serving.

Variations

BLACK PEPPER RANCH

Add a generous spoonful of freshly ground black pepper.

CHEESE RANCH

Add some freshly grated Parmesan cheese or crumbled blue cheese.

CUCUMBER RANCH

Grate ¼ to ½ cup fresh cucumber and let it sit in a strainer for a few minutes, pressing gently to encourage excess juices to drip out, then stir it into the dressing and adjust the seasonings to taste.

HORSERADISH RANCH

Add a little grated fresh or prepared horseradish to taste for a subtly spicy effect.

LOW-FAT RANCH

Note that most buttermilk sold today is low in fat; to make a low-fat dressing, use reduced- or nonfat mayonnaise.

Thousand Island Dressing

1 cup mayonnaise

¼ cup ketchup

¼ cup sweet pickled cucumber relish

In a mixing bowl, stir together the mayonnaise, ketchup, and relish until thoroughly blended. Cover the bowl with plastic wrap and refrigerate until serving time.

TEST KITCHEN NOTES

MAYBE THE NAME REFERS TO THE MYRIAD CHOPPED BITS SUSPENDED IN THE DRESSING'S CREAMY BASE. WHILE SOME RECIPES CALL FOR FANCIER FLOURISHES LIKE TOMATO-CHILI SAUCE AND CHOPPED OLIVES, I PREFER MY THOUSAND ISLAND DRESSING THE OLD-FASHIONED WAY, WITH KETCHUP AND SWEET PICKLE RELISH. FOR A LOWER-FAT VERSION, USE REDUCED-FAT MAYONNAISE, OR SUBSTITUTE LOW-FAT OR NONFAT PLAIN YOGURT FOR SOME OF THE MAYO.

THIS DRESSING WORKS VERY WELL WITH BASIC LETTUCE-BASED MEAT, POULTRY, AND SEAFOOD SALADS.

Russian Dressing

MAKES ABOUT 1½ CUPS

½ cup vegetable oil

½ cup ketchup

¼ cup lemon juice

2 tablespoons sugar

1 tablespoon Worcestershire sauce

1 teaspoon dry mustard powder

Salt

Black pepper

Put all the ingredients except the salt and pepper in a jar with a tight-fitting lid and shake vigorously until well blended. Taste the dressing; stir in salt and pepper to taste. Cover and refrigerate until serving time.

TEST KITCHEN NOTES

RUSSIAN DRESSING GOES PARTICULARLY WELL WITH MEAT AND SEAFOOD SALADS.

CHAPTER 3

Classics and Variations

L ike legendary stars, some main-dish salads are recognizable by a single name: Caesar, Cobb, Waldorf, Niçoise. They've no doubt achieved such status at least in part because of their singular power to satisfy. Nothing satiates the senses quite like a rich, garlicky Caesar; contrasts tastes and textures like a Cobb; refreshes the palate like a Waldorf; or combines lightness and heartiness quite like a Niçoise.

Another way such classics resemble true stars is their versatility—the many ways in which they can take on a wide range of different guises while retaining their inimitable identities. On the pages that follow, you'll witness this phenomenon again and again, with variations that offer refreshing updates of the reliable standards. After you've sampled a few of them, don't hesitate to try your hand at variations of your own. You might well create a new star.

Classic Caesar Salad

SERVES 4

DRESSING

2 garlic cloves, peeled
4 oil-packed anchovy fillets
3 tablespoons lemon juice
1 tablespoon Worcestershire sauce
½ teaspoon dry mustard powder
2 eggs
½ cup extra-virgin olive oil

SALAD

2 large heads romaine, leaves separated, washed, and chilled
2 cups Garlic Croutons (see page 18)
½ cup finely grated fresh Parmesan cheese
16 oil-packed anchovy fillets

1. First, make the dressing. Bring a small saucepan of water to a boil over medium-high heat. Meanwhile, one at a time, put the garlic cloves in a garlic press and press them into a large salad bowl. Add the 4 anchovy fillets and, with the tines of a fork, mash them together with the pressed garlic until they form a smooth paste. Stirring briskly with a small wire whisk, add the lemon juice and Worcestershire sauce. Add the mustard powder and stir until it is completely dissolved.

2. When the water is boiling, gently drop in the eggs and boil them for precisely 1 minute. Drain immediately and rinse under cold running water until the eggs are just cool enough to handle. Break the eggs carefully into the salad bowl, using a small teaspoon to scoop them out if necessary. Whisk the eggs into the other ingredients just until blended. Then, whisking continuously, pour in the olive oil in a slow, steady stream.

3. Remove the lettuce leaves from the refrigerator and reserve several of the largest outer leaves to garnish each serving. Tear the remaining leaves into bite-size pieces, dropping them into the salad bowl; you should have about 16 cups in all. Add the croutons and sprinkle in the Parmesan cheese. If you like, add the whole anchovies; or leave them out, reserving them to garnish individual servings for those who want them. Toss the salad thoroughly with the dressing.

4. Arrange the reserved romaine around the edges of large, chilled, individual serving plates or bowls. Pile the salad on top. Garnish with any reserved anchovies and serve immediately.

TEST KITCHEN NOTES

WHO COULD HAVE IMAGINED THAT THE SALAD THROWN TOGETHER TO PLEASE A GROUP OF REVELERS IN TIJUANA, MEXICO, ON THE JULY 4TH WEEKEND IN 1924 BY CAESAR CARDINI, AN ITALIAN-BORN CHEF, WOULD BECOME ONE OF THE WORLD'S GREATEST SALADS? THE BORDER TOWN, JUST SOUTH OF SAN DIEGO, CALIFORNIA, WAS A FASHIONABLE GETAWAY FOR STARS OF THE GROWING MOVIE INDUSTRY, WHO OVER THE COMING DECADES MADE CAESAR'S CREATION THE "IN" SALAD AT THEIR OWN FAVORITE WATERING HOLES.

KEEPING ITS ROOTS IN MIND, THE LIST OF DRESSING INGREDIENTS READS LIKE A BRACING HANGOVER CURE: GARLIC, ANCHOVIES, MUSTARD, WORCESTERSHIRE SAUCE, AND BARELY COOKED EGGS. IF YOU'RE LEERY OF THOSE EGGS BECAUSE OF RECENT SCARES ABOUT SALMONELLA, YOU COULD INSTEAD SOFT-BOIL THEM FOR 3 TO 4 MINUTES AND USE JUST THE STILL-OOZING YOLKS. OR SUBSTITUTE A COUPLE TABLESPOONS OF HEAVY CREAM, WHICH WILL GIVE A SIMILARLY RICH CONSISTENCY AND FLAVOR.

IF YOU BUY PREGRATED PARMESAN, BE SURE THAT YOU CHOOSE ONE THAT CONSISTS OF NOTHING BUT PURE, IMPORTED ITALIAN PARMESAN. AND MAKE SURE THE GRATED CHEESE YOU BUY IS GRATED INTO FINE PARTICLES SO THAT IT BLENDS PROPERLY WITH THE OTHER CAESAR SALAD INGREDIENTS.

Light Caesar Salad with Grilled Shrimp

SERVES 4

GRILLED SHRIMP

1 pound extra-large shrimp, peeled and
    deveined
2 tablespoons lemon juice
2 tablespoons extra-virgin olive oil
Salt
White pepper

DRESSING

3 garlic cloves, peeled
4 oil-packed anchovy fillets, well drained
3 tablespoons lemon juice
1 tablespoon Worcestershire sauce
½ teaspoon dry mustard powder
3 tablespoons yogurt
½ cup extra-virgin olive oil

SALAD

2 large heads romaine, leaves separated,
    washed, and chilled
2 cups Fat-free Garlic Croutons
    (see page 18)
½ cup freshly grated Parmesan cheese
16 oil-packed anchovy fillets, well drained

1. Preheat the grill or broiler. In a bowl, toss the shrimp together with the lemon juice and olive oil and leave them to marinate while you make the dressing.

2. One at a time, put the garlic cloves in a garlic press and press them into a large salad bowl. Add the 4 anchovy fillets and, with the tines of a fork, mash them together with the pressed garlic until they form a smooth paste. Stirring briskly with a small wire whisk, add the lemon juice and Worcestershire sauce. Add the mustard powder and stir until it is completely dissolved. Whisk the yogurt into the other ingredients just until blended. Then, whisking continuously, pour in the olive oil in a slow, steady stream.

3. Remove the shrimp from the marinade and discard the marinade. Season the shrimp all over to taste with salt and white pepper and put them on the grill or under the broiler, cooking them just until uniformly pink and firm, about 2 minutes per side.

4. While the shrimp cook, assemble the salad. Remove the lettuce leaves from the refrigerator and reserve several of the largest outer leaves to garnish each serving. Tear the remaining leaves into bite-size pieces, dropping them into the salad bowl; you should have about 16 cups in all. Add the croutons and sprinkle in the Parmesan. If you like, add the whole anchovies; or leave them out, reserving them to garnish individual servings for those who want them. Toss the salad thoroughly, until all the lettuce is well coated with the dressing and cheese.

5. Arrange the reserved romaine leaves around the edges of large, chilled, individual serving plates or bowls. Pile the salad on top. Garnish with any reserved anchovies and top with the grilled shrimp. Serve immediately.

TEST KITCHEN NOTES

IN AN AGE OF HEALTH-CONSCIOUS, LOW-FAT COOKING AND EATING, IT'S INEVITABLE THAT THE CAESAR SALAD WOULD COME UNDER SOME SCRUTINY, CONSIDERING ALL ITS EGGS, OLIVE OIL, AND CHEESE.

THIS RECIPE REMARKABLY APPROXIMATES THE CLASSIC CAESAR, WHILE CUTTING OUT MUCH OF THE FAT. THE SECRET IS USING PLAIN NONFAT YOGURT TO GIVE THE DRESSING BODY AND RICHNESS. I ALSO ADD A LITTLE BIT OF OLIVE OIL FOR FLAVOR; BE SURE TO USE A GOOD EXTRA-VIRGIN OIL THAT HAS A DISTINCTIVE OLIVE TASTE.

WITH ITS SPRIGHTLY FLAVORS, I FIND THAT THIS PARTICULAR VERSION OF CAESAR SALAD GOES VERY WELL WITH A FEW QUICKLY GRILLED OR BROILED PIECES OF SWORDFISH, SALMON, OR AHI TUNA.

Cajun Caesar Salad with Blackened Steak

SERVES 4

BLACKENED STEAK

2 tablespoons extra-virgin olive oil

4 teaspoons Cajun-style blackened spice
  blend or to taste

4 tenderloin or filet mignon steaks (about
  6 ounces each), well trimmed of fat

DRESSING

4 garlic cloves, peeled

4 oil-packed anchovy fillets, well drained

3 tablespoons lemon juice

1 tablespoon Worcestershire sauce

1 teaspoon hot red pepper sauce,
  such as Tabasco

½ teaspoon dry mustard powder

2 eggs

½ cup extra-virgin olive oil

SALAD

2 large heads romaine, leaves separated,
  washed, and chilled

2 cups Garlic-Spice Croutons
  (see page 18)

½ cup freshly grated Parmesan cheese

1. Preheat the grill or broiler. In a bowl, use a fork to stir together the olive oil and Cajun spices to form a paste. Add the steaks, turning them in the paste and smearing them evenly with it. Leave them to marinate at room temperature while you make the dressing.

2. Bring a small saucepan of water to a boil over medium-high heat. Meanwhile, one at a time, put the garlic cloves in a garlic press and press them into a large salad bowl. Add the 4 anchovy fillets and, with the tines of a fork, mash them together with the garlic until they form a smooth paste. Stirring briskly with a small wire whisk, add the lemon juice, Worcestershire sauce, and hot pepper sauce. Add the mustard powder and stir until dissolved.

3. When the water is boiling, gently drop in the eggs and boil them for precisely 1 minute. Drain immediately and rinse under cold running water until the eggs are just cool enough to handle. Break the eggs carefully into the salad bowl, using a small teaspoon to scoop them out if necessary. Whisk the eggs into

the other ingredients just until blended. Then, whisking continuously, pour in the olive oil in a slow, steady stream.

4. Put the steaks coated with their spice paste on the grill or under the broiler. Cook them to your liking, about 4 minutes per side for medium-rare.

5. While the steaks cook, assemble the salad. Remove the lettuce leaves from the refrigerator, reserving several large outer leaves as garnish. Tear the remaining leaves into bite-size pieces, dropping them into the salad bowl; you should have about 16 cups. Add the croutons and sprinkle in the Parmesan. Toss the salad thoroughly, until well coated with the dressing and cheese.

6. Arrange the reserved whole leaves on large, chilled, individual serving plates. Pile the salad on top. Cut each steak crosswise into ½-inch-thick slices and arrange them on top of the salads, drizzling any juices from the cutting board over the meat. Serve immediately.

TEST KITCHEN NOTES

THE CLASSIC CAESAR HAS ALWAYS HAD AN UNSPOKEN REPUTATION AS A ROBUST SALAD. THIS RECIPE UPS THE ANTE BY ADDING MORE GARLIC AND A SHOT OF HOT PEPPER SAUCE IN THE DRESSING AND TOPPING IT WITH WELL-SEASONED STEAK.

Southwestern Caesar Salad with Chipotle Chicken Breast

SERVES 4

CHIPOTLE CHICKEN BREAST

1 can (about 7 ounces) chipotle chilies in sauce
4 boneless, skinless chicken breast halves (4 to 6 ounces each)
Salt
Black pepper

DRESSING

3 garlic cloves, peeled
4 oil-packed anchovy fillets, well drained
3 tablespoons lemon juice
1 tablespoon Worcestershire sauce
½ teaspoon dry mustard powder
2 eggs
½ cup extra-virgin olive oil

SALAD

2 large heads romaine, leaves separated, washed, and chilled
1 large bag (about 10 ounces) tortilla chips
½ cup freshly grated Parmesan cheese

1. Preheat the grill or broiler. In a bowl, use a fork to mash together the chipotles with their sauce until they form a coarse paste. Add the chicken breasts, coating them evenly with the paste. Leave them to marinate at room temperature while you make the dressing.

2. Bring a small saucepan of water to a boil over medium-high heat. Meanwhile, one at a time, put the garlic cloves in a garlic press and press them into a large salad bowl. Add the 4 anchovy fillets and, with the tines of a fork, mash them together with the garlic to form a smooth paste. Stirring briskly with a small wire whisk, add the lemon juice and Worcestershire sauce. Add the mustard powder and stir until dissolved.

3. Gently drop the eggs in the boiling water and boil precisely 1 minute. Drain immediately and rinse under cold running water until the eggs are just cool enough to handle. Break the eggs into the salad bowl, using a teaspoon to scoop them out if necessary. Whisk the eggs into the other ingredients just until blended. Then, whisking continuously, pour in the olive oil in a slow, steady stream.

4. Remove the chicken breasts from their chipotle marinade and, depending on how intensely spiced you want them, wipe off some or most of the paste, discarding it. Season the chicken breasts all over to taste with salt and pepper and put them on the grill or under the broiler. Cook them just until uniformly done, about 5 minutes per side.

5. While the chicken breasts cook, assemble the salad. Remove the lettuce leaves from the refrigerator. Discard any tough, large outer leaves and tear the remaining leaves into bite-size pieces, dropping them into the salad bowl; you should have about 16 cups. Add three quarters of the tortilla chips, breaking them coarsely into bite-size pieces; sprinkle in the Parmesan. Toss the salad thoroughly with the dressing.

6. Pile the salad on top of large, chilled, individual serving plates or bowls. Arrange the remaining chips around each salad. Cut each chicken breast crosswise into ½-inch-thick slices and arrange them on top of the salads. Serve immediately.

TEST KITCHEN NOTES

THE STRONG FLAVORS OF CAESAR SALAD STAND UP VERY WELL TO THE SMOKY INTENSITY OF THE CHILI-MARINATED CHICKEN.

AFTER HANDLING CHILI PEPPERS, TAKE CARE TO WASH YOUR HANDS THOROUGHLY WITH WARM, SOAPY WATER, AND AVOID TOUCHING YOUR EYES OR ANY CUTS OR OTHER SENSITIVE AREAS.

Roast Beef and Bitter Greens Cobb with Balsamic Blue Cheese Vinaigrette

SERVES 4

DRESSING

6 tablespoons balsamic vinegar

¼ pound blue cheese, crumbled

¼ tablespoon salt

2 teaspoons dried oregano

¾ cup extra-virgin olive oil

SALAD

4 eggs

¾ pound smoked bacon, thinly sliced

16 cups (about 2 pounds) mixed arugula, radicchio, chicory, endive, or romaine

4 Roma tomatoes

2 ripe avocados, preferably Haas variety

2 tablespoons lemon juice

1 pound leftover cooked beef, cut into ½-inch chunks

1. First, make the dressing. In a mixing bowl, use a fork to stir together the balsamic vinegar, blue cheese, and salt until the salt dissolves completely and the cheese slightly. With your fingertips, crumble in the oregano and stir briefly to combine. Stirring briskly, slowly pour in the olive oil until fully incorporated. Set the dressing aside.

2. Put the eggs in a saucepan of cold water and bring to a boil over medium-high heat. As soon as the water starts to boil, check the time and cook the eggs 10 minutes. Drain well, rinse with cold running water, and set the eggs aside.

3. While the eggs are boiling, cook the bacon. Arrange the strips side by side in one or two frying pans and cook over medium heat, turning frequently, until crisp and brown, about 10 minutes. Remove the bacon and set aside to drain on several layers of paper toweling.

4. With your fingers, tear the salad leaves into small, bite-size pieces. Arrange the leaves in an even bed in a large salad bowl or large individual serving bowls.

5. Cut out and discard the tough cores of the tomatoes. Cut them in half and, with a finger, poke out the seeds. Coarsely chop the tomatoes and arrange in a neat section atop the salad.

6. Halve, pit, and peel the avocados. Cut them into bite-size chunks, put them in a small bowl, and gently toss with the lemon juice to coat. Arrange the avocado in a neat section atop the leaves.

7. Peel the eggs and coarsely chop them. Arrange the eggs in another section atop the leaves.

8. Crumble the bacon into small, bite-size pieces and arrange them atop the leaves.

9. Finally, arrange the beef chunks on top of the leaves.

10. Present the large salad or individual portions at the table, passing the dressing alongside. Alternatively, dress and toss the salad in the kitchen before serving.

TEST KITCHEN NOTES

THINK OF THIS AS A BEEF-EATER'S COBB, WITH MORE ROBUST-TASTING BITTER GREENS FORMING THE BACKDROP FOR THE MEAT. IT'S A PARTICULARLY GOOD WAY TO USE UP LEFTOVER ROAST BEEF OR GRILLED STEAK FROM THE PREVIOUS NIGHT'S DINNER.

I'VE TAKEN THE LIBERTY OF ADDING THE BLUE CHEESE TO THE DRESSING. FOR AN ESPECIALLY RICH EFFECT, SUBSTITUTE IMPORTED ITALIAN GORGONZOLA CHEESE.

Classic Cobb Salad

DRESSING

¼ cup lemon juice
½ teaspoon salt
½ teaspoon white pepper
½ teaspoon sugar
2 tablespoons Dijon mustard
¾ cup extra-virgin olive oil

SALAD

4 eggs
¾ pound smoked bacon, thinly sliced
2 large heads romaine, leaves separated,
     washed, and chilled
4 large Roma tomatoes
2 ripe avocados, preferably Haas variety
2 tablespoons lemon juice
1 pound cooked turkey breast, cut into
     ½-inch chunks
½ pound blue cheese, crumbled

1. First, make the dressing. In a mixing bowl, use a fork or small wire whisk to stir together the lemon juice, salt, pepper, and sugar until the salt and sugar dissolve. Stir in the mustard until smooth. Stirring briskly, slowly pour in the olive oil until fully incorporated. Set the dressing aside.

2. Put the eggs in a saucepan of cold water and bring to a boil over medium-high heat. As soon as the water starts to boil, check the time and cook the eggs 10 minutes. Drain well, rinse with cold running water, and set the eggs aside.

3. While the eggs are boiling, cook the bacon. Arrange the strips side by side in one or two frying pans and cook over medium heat, turning frequently, until crisp and brown, about 10 minutes. Remove the bacon and set aside to drain on several layers of paper toweling.

4. Remove the lettuce leaves from the refrigerator, discarding any large, tough, outer leaves. With your fingers or with a sharp knife, break or cut the lettuce into small, bite-size pieces; you should have about 16 cups. Arrange the lettuce in an even bed in a large salad bowl or large individual serving bowls.

5. Cut out and discard the tough cores of the tomatoes. Cut them in half and, with a finger, poke out the seeds. Coarsely chop the tomatoes and arrange in a neat section atop the salad.

6. Halve, pit, and peel the avocados. Cut them into bite-size chunks, put them in a small bowl, and gently toss with the lemon juice to coat. Arrange the avocado in a neat section atop the lettuce.

7. Peel the eggs and cut them into sections. Arrange the eggs in another area atop the lettuce.

8. Crumble the bacon into small, bite-size pieces and arrange them atop the lettuce.

9. Finally, arrange the turkey pieces and the blue cheese on top of the lettuce.

10. Present the large salad or individual portions at the table, passing the dressing alongside. Alternatively, dress and toss the salad in the kitchen before serving.

TEST KITCHEN NOTES

BOB COBB OF HOLLYWOOD'S LEGENDARY BROWN DERBY RESTAURANT CAME UP WITH THIS NOW-CLASSIC SALAD BACK IN 1936. ITS ENDURING APPEAL LIES, I THINK, IN THE WEALTH OF SENSORY EXPERIENCES IT OFFERS IN A SINGLE BOWL.

WHEN PRESENTING A COBB SALAD, MANY PEOPLE ENJOY THE BEAUTIFUL CONTRASTS OF COLOR AND SHAPE THAT COME FROM THE VARIOUS INGREDIENTS ATOP THE BED OF LETTUCE. BUT THAT LEAVES YOU HAVING TO TOSS THE ENTIRE SALAD OR INDIVIDUAL SERVINGS AT THE TABLE, A MESSY PROSPECT. I RECOMMEND PRETOSSING THE SALAD IN THE KITCHEN BEFORE SERVING.

Thai Cobb Salad with Chicken and Ginger-Mint Dressing

SERVES 4

DRESSING

6 tablespoons seasoned rice vinegar

1½ tablespoons finely minced
   fresh ginger

1 tablespoon soy sauce

2 teaspoons sugar

1 tablespoon finely chopped fresh
   mint leaves

½ cup vegetable oil

SALAD

4 eggs

16 cups (about 2 pounds) baby butter
   lettuce leaves or mixed salad greens

4 Roma tomatoes

1 cup cooked chicken meat, cut into
   ½-inch chunks

½ pound char siu (Chinese barbecued
   pork), cut into ¼-inch dice

½ pound mozzarella, Monterey Jack,
   or fontina cheese, cut into
   ½-inch cubes

4 pickling-style cucumbers, cut into
   ½-inch chunks

½ cup dry-roasted peanuts

4 sprigs fresh mint, for garnish

1. First, make the dressing. In a mixing bowl, use a fork or small wire whisk to stir together the rice vinegar, ginger, soy sauce, and sugar until the sugar dissolves. Stir in the mint. Stirring briskly, slowly pour in the vegetable oil until fully incorporated. Set the dressing aside.

2. Put the eggs in a saucepan of cold water and bring to a boil over medium-high heat. As soon as the water starts to boil, check the time and cook the eggs 10 minutes. Drain well, rinse with cold running water, and set the eggs aside.

3. Arrange the lettuce leaves in an even bed in a large salad bowl or large individual serving bowls.

4. Cut out and discard the tough cores of the tomatoes. Cut each in half and, with a finger, poke out the seeds. Coarsely chop the tomatoes and arrange in a neat section atop the salad.

5. Peel the eggs and coarsely chop them. Arrange the eggs in another section atop the lettuce.

6. Arrange the chicken, *char siu*, cheese, and cucumbers on top of the lettuce. Scatter the peanuts on top. Garnish with mint sprigs.

7. Present the large salad or individual portions at the table, passing the dressing alongside. Alternatively, dress and toss the salad in the kitchen before serving.

TEST KITCHEN NOTES

As a passionate baseball fan, I could not resist the reference to the legendary player. That was just the starting point for this Cobb variation, though—it wouldn't be here now if it didn't work.

The salad, in fact, is based on traditional Southeast Asian dishes. What all these dishes have in common is a dressing that pulls the salad together in an eye-opening way.

In place of the bacon traditionally used in Cobb salads, I call here for *char siu*, Chinese-style barbecued pork. You'll find this lean, meaty, sweetly spiced cooked pork in Asian markets, and you might even be able to get a portion "to go" from a local Chinese restaurant. Alternatively, use thickly sliced honey-cured cooked ham; or go with sugar-cured bacon.

Greek Shrimp and Spinach Cobb Salad

SERVES 4

DRESSING

Lemon Vinaigrette (see page 25)

SALAD

4 eggs

½ pound smoked bacon, thinly sliced

16 cups (about 2 pounds) packed baby
    spinach leaves, thoroughly washed
    and patted dry

2 red bell peppers, quartered, stemmed,
    seeded, and ribbed

2 ripe avocados, preferably Haas variety

2 tablespoons lemon juice

1 pound steamed baby shrimp

½ pound feta cheese, crumbled

¼ cup pine nuts, toasted (see page 17)

1. Prepare the dressing and set it aside.

2. Put the eggs in a saucepan of cold water and bring to a boil over medium-high heat. As soon as the water starts to boil, check the time and cook the eggs 10 minutes. Drain well, rinse with cold running water, and set the eggs aside.

3. While the eggs are boiling, cook the bacon. Arrange the strips side by side in one or two frying pans and cook over medium heat, turning frequently, until crisp and brown, about 10 minutes. Remove the bacon and set aside to drain on several layers of paper toweling.

4. Arrange the spinach in an even bed in a large salad bowl or large individual serving bowls.

5. Cut the bell pepper quarters in half lengthwise. Then cut them crosswise into strips about ¼ inch thick. Arrange the peppers in sections atop the spinach.

6. Halve, pit, and peel the avocados. Cut them into bite-size chunks, put them in a small bowl, and gently toss with the lemon juice to coat. Arrange the avocado in a neat section atop the spinach.

7. Peel the eggs and coarsely chop them. Arrange the eggs in another section atop the spinach.

8. Crumble the bacon into small, bite-size pieces and arrange them atop the spinach.

9. Finally, arrange the shrimp and the feta cheese on top of the spinach. Garnish with pine nuts.

10. Present the large salad or individual portions at the table, passing the dressing alongside. Alternatively, dress and toss the salad in the kitchen before serving.

TEST KITCHEN NOTES

ALTHOUGH THIS VARIATION MIGHT LOOK AND TASTE DIFFERENT FROM THE CLASSIC COBB, IT DOES FOLLOW THE BASIC FORMULA.

BABY SPINACH LEAVES REPLACE THE ROMAINE. IN A PINCH, YOU COULD SUBSTITUTE LITTLE BUTTER LETTUCE LEAVES, OR STICK WITH THE CLASSIC ROMAINE. PRECOOKED BABY SHRIMP TAKE THE PLACE OF THE TURKEY OR CHICKEN. THAT'S A SIMPLE SWAP OF ONE PROTEIN FOR ANOTHER. YOU COULD ALSO TRY PRECOOKED CAREFULLY SORTED LUMP CRABMEAT. STANDING IN FOR THE TOMATO ARE STRIPS OF RED BELL PEPPER, WHICH ALSO REPLACE SOME OF THE CRISPNESS LACKING IN THE SPINACH. YOU COULD, HOWEVER, STICK WITH TOMATO IF YOU PREFER. AND FETA CHEESE ASSUMES THE ROLE OF A COBB'S BLUE CHEESE.

Classic Waldorf Salad with Poached Chicken

SERVES 4

2 cups chicken broth

1 pound boneless, skinless chicken
    breasts

4 apples

¼ cup lemon juice

4 stalks celery, cut into ½-inch-wide
    pieces

1 cup shelled walnut halves or pieces,
    toasted (see page 17)

¼ cup finely snipped fresh chives

1⅓ cups mayonnaise

4 cups radicchio or butter lettuce leaves,
    for presentation

1. In a medium-size saucepan, bring the broth to a boil over medium-high heat. Add the chicken breasts, reduce the heat to low, and simmer gently, covered, until the chicken is cooked through, about 10 minutes. Let the chicken cool to room temperature in the broth; reserve the broth, if you wish, and transfer the chicken to a bowl, cover, and refrigerate until cold.

2. Quarter and core the apples and cut them into ½-inch chunks. Immediately put them in a large mixing bowl and toss with the lemon juice to coat them well to prevent them from discoloring.

3. Cut or tear the chicken into ½-inch chunks and add them to the bowl. Add the celery pieces.

4. Reserve several of the most attractive walnut halves or pieces to garnish the salad. Add the remainder to the bowl along with the chives and the mayonnaise. Toss well to mix and coat the ingredients. If you plan to serve the salad later, cover with plastic wrap and refrigerate.

5. Arrange the radicchio or butter lettuce leaves to form a bed on large, chilled, individual serving plates or shallow bowls. Mound the salad mixture in the center and garnish with the reserved nuts.

TEST KITCHEN NOTES

OSCAR TSCHIRKY, MAÎTRE D'HÔTEL OF THE WALDORF-ASTORIA HOTEL IN NEW YORK, DEVELOPED THIS CLASSIC SALAD IN THE LATE 1890S. THE NOW-STANDARD WALNUTS THAT MOST PEOPLE FIND SUCH A PLEASING PART OF IT WERE ADDED LATER, FIRST APPEARING IN PRINT AROUND 1928.

WITH ITS SWEETNESS, CRISPNESS, AND THE MILD RICHNESS OF A MAYONNAISE DRESSING, THE WALDORF RAPIDLY FOUND FAVOR AS A LIGHT LUNCHEON SPECIALTY. I ADMIT TO HAVING TAKEN THE VERY SLIGHT LIBERTY HERE OF ADDING THE SORT OF POACHED CHICKEN THAT NO DOUBT OFTEN ACCOMPANIED THIS SALAD ON EARLY MENUS.

FOR EFFECT, CHOOSE A RED-SKINNED, FAIRLY CRISP EATING APPLE SUCH AS A MCINTOSH, JONATHAN, OR WINESAP. YOU COULD ALSO, IF YOU WISH, USE A MIXTURE OF RED APPLES AND GREEN OR YELLOW VARIETIES SUCH AS GOLDEN DELICIOUS, GRANNY SMITH, OR JONAGOLD.

Waldorf Salad with Pears, Prosciutto, Gruyère, Hazelnuts, and Orange Mayonnaise

SERVES 4

6 large pears
½ cup orange juice
4 stalks celery, cut into ½-inch-wide
    pieces
1 cup hazelnuts, toasted (see page 17)
    and skins rubbed off
¼ pound prosciutto, cut into thin strips
2 tablespoons finely chopped fresh mint
    leaves
1 cup mayonnaise
4 cups mixed baby salad greens
1 head Belgian endive, leaves separated
Fresh mint sprigs, for garnish

1. Quarter and core the pears. Cut 4 of them into ½-inch chunks and the remainder into slender lengthwise wedges. Immediately put all the pear pieces in a large mixing bowl and toss gently with the orange juice to coat them well to prevent them from discoloring. Remove the wedges and set them aside.

2. Add the celery to the pear chunks along with the hazelnuts, prosciutto, and chopped mint. Add the mayonnaise and toss well to mix and coat the ingredients. If you plan to serve the salad later, cover with plastic wrap and refrigerate.

3. Arrange the mixed greens to form a bed on large, chilled, individual serving plates or shallow bowls. Mound the salad mixture in the center and arrange the pear wedges and Belgian endive leaves around it. Garnish with mint sprigs.

Summer Fruit Waldorf Salad with Pecans and Baby Shrimp

SERVES 4

2 pounds freestone peaches

1 pound plums

1 pound cherries

4 stalks celery, cut into ½-inch-wide
    pieces

¼ cup lemon juice

1 tablespoon finely grated lemon zest

1 cup shelled pecan halves or pieces,
    toasted (see page 17)

1 pound cooked baby bay shrimp

1 cup mayonnaise

8 cups butter lettuce leaves

Fresh mint sprigs, for garnish

1. With a sharp knife, halve the peaches and plums, remove their pits, and cut the fruit into ½- to 1-inch chunks. Set aside a few attractive pieces for garnishing and put the remainder into a large mixing bowl.

2. Reserve several attractive whole cherries with stems for garnishing. With a small, sharp knife, halve the remainder and remove their pits. Put the cherry halves in the bowl with the other fruit.

3. Add the celery to the bowl along with the lemon juice and zest. Toss well to coat all the ingredients.

4. Set aside a few attractive pecan halves or pieces and put the remainder into the bowl. Add the bay shrimp and the mayonnaise and toss well to mix and coat the ingredients. If you plan to serve the salad later, cover with plastic wrap and refrigerate.

5. Arrange the butter lettuce leaves to form a bed on large, chilled, individual serving plates or shallow bowls. Mound the salad mixture in the center and garnish with the reserved fruit pieces, nuts, and mint sprigs.

TEST KITCHEN NOTES

WHAT A REFRESHING SURPRISE THIS WALDORF SALAD VARIATION IS, ESPECIALLY IF YOU, AS I DO, LOVE SUMMER FRUIT. IF YOU TAKE CARE TO SELECT FRUIT THAT IS ABSOLUTELY RIPE YET STILL FIRM ENOUGH TO BE CUT UP AND HOLD ITS SHAPE, THE SALAD WILL HAVE A JEWELLIKE BEAUTY, AND EVERY BITE WILL BE FILLED WITH SWEET JUICE.

USE THE ACCOMPANYING INGREDIENT QUANTITIES ONLY AS A STARTING POINT FOR YOUR OWN VARIATIONS. IF YOU ESPECIALLY LIKE CHERRIES, USE MORE, PARTICULARLY IF SOME RARE VARIETY LIKE THE INCREDIBLE BLUSHING GOLDEN RAINIER CHERRIES IS AVAILABLE. INCLUDE SOME NECTARINES IN PLACE OF THE PEACHES, IF YOU WISH. I FIND THE TARTNESS OF SOME PLUMS' SKIN A BRACING CONTRAST TO THE OTHER FLAVORS; BUT IF THEY DISTRACT YOU, PEEL THE PLUMS, OR LEAVE THEM OUT ENTIRELY. AND DON'T BOTHER PEELING THE PEACHES UNLESS THEIR SKINS ARE SO FUZZY AS TO SPOIL YOUR PLEASURE.

Classic Salade Niçoise

SERVES 4

DRESSING

2 tablespoons white wine vinegar

1 teaspoon lemon juice

¼ teaspoon salt

¼ teaspoon sugar

1 tablespoon Dijon mustard

6 tablespoons extra-virgin olive oil

SALAD

¾ pound boiling potatoes

4 eggs

½ pound thin green beans, trimmed and
    cut into pieces about 1½ inches long

2 tablespoons capers, drained

4 Roma tomatoes, cut into thin wedges

¼ pound Niçoise cured olives, halved
    and pitted

2 cans (about 6 ounces each) Italian-style
    oil-packed tuna, drained

1 tin (2 ounces) oil-packed anchovy
    fillets, drained (optional)

1 tablespoon finely chopped fresh chives

1 tablespoon finely chopped parsley

2 heads butter lettuce, leaves separated

1. First, make the dressing. In a small bowl, use a fork or small wire whisk to stir together the vinegar, lemon juice, salt, and sugar until the salt and sugar dissolve. Stir in the mustard until blended. Stirring briskly, pour in the oil in a thin, steady stream. Set aside.

2. Put the potatoes in a saucepan with lightly salted cold water to cover. Bring to a boil over medium-high heat and cook until tender when pierced with the tip of a small, sharp knife, 15 to 20 minutes.

At the same time, put the eggs in another saucepan of cold water and bring to a boil over medium-high heat. As soon as the water starts to boil, check the time and cook the eggs for 10 minutes. Drain well, rinse with cold running water, and set the eggs aside.

Drain and peel the potatoes while still hot. Let them cool, then cut into ½-inch cubes and place in a mixing bowl.

3. Meanwhile, bring yet another saucepan of salted water to a boil over medium-high heat. Add the green beans and cook until tender-crisp, 3 to 4 minutes. Drain and rinse under cold running water until cool. Drain well and add to the potatoes.

4. Add the capers, tomatoes, olives, tuna, and, if you like, the anchovies to the mixing bowl. Scatter with the chives and parsley.

Pour the dressing over the salad ingredients and toss gently but well until evenly coated.

5. Arrange the butter lettuce leaves on individual serving plates to form attractive beds. Spoon the salad mixture onto the beds of lettuce.

TEST KITCHEN NOTES

SOME PEOPLE LIKE TO ARRANGE THE FEATURED INGREDIENTS NEATLY ON TOP OF THE BED OF LETTUCE. I FEEL, HOWEVER, THAT SALADE NIÇOISE HAS A COMFORTABLE INFORMALITY THAT CALLS FOR IT TO BE TOSSED, AS HERE, AND I RESERVE THE MORE STYLIZED PRESENTATIONS FOR THE FRESH-FISH VARIATIONS THAT FOLLOW.

Salade Niçoise with Seared Fresh Tuna, Fresh Mozzarella, and Beefsteak Tomato

SERVES 4

DRESSING

¼ cup lemon juice

2 teaspoons sugar

1½ tablespoons Dijon mustard

¾ cup extra-virgin olive oil

SALAD

4 fillets fresh ahi tuna (about 4 ounces each)

2 tablespoons extra-virgin olive oil

2 tablespoons lemon juice

4 eggs

6 ounces arugula

2 beefsteak tomatoes
    (about 10 ounces each)

1 pound mozzarella cheese, preferably
    buffalo mozzarella

Salt

Black pepper

1 tablespoon capers, drained

¼ pound Niçoise olives, drained

4 tablespoons finely shredded fresh
    basil leaves

1. First, make the dressing. In a small bowl, use a fork or small wire whisk to stir together the lemon juice and sugar until the sugar dissolves. Stir in the mustard until blended. Stirring briskly, pour in the oil in a thin, steady stream until fully incorporated. Set aside.

2. Put the ahi tuna fillets in a shallow bowl large enough to hold them in a single layer. Add the olive oil and lemon juice, turn the fillets to coat them, and leave at room temperature to marinate.

3. Preheat the broiler or grill.

4. Put the eggs in a saucepan of cold water and bring to a boil over medium-high heat. As soon as the water starts to boil, check the time and cook the eggs 10 minutes. Drain well, rinse with cold running water, and set the eggs aside.

5. Toss the arugula leaves with a few spoonfuls of the dressing and arrange them in a bed on one side of four serving plates.

6. With a small, sharp knife, cut out the cores of the tomatoes. Cut the tomatoes in half through their stem ends, then cut them crosswise into ¼-inch-thick slices. Cut the mozzarella into slices of the same thickness. Arrange the tomato and cheese slices overlapping across the other half of each plate and spoon some more of the dressing over them.

7. Shell the hard-boiled eggs, cut them into quarters, and arrange them on each plate.

8. Season the tuna fillets with salt and black pepper and cook them on the grill or under the broiler just until nicely seared, about 2 minutes per side. Cut each fillet crosswise into slices about ½ inch thick and array them atop the beds of arugula.

9. Spoon more dressing liberally over the tomatoes and mozzarella and on top of the tuna. Garnish with the capers, olives, and fresh basil and serve immediately.

TEST KITCHEN NOTES

THE COOKING INSTRUCTIONS GIVEN PRODUCE TUNA THAT IS SEARED—THAT IS, COOKED AROUND THE EDGES AND STILL ROSY PINK IN THE MIDDLE. YOU MAY, IF YOU WISH, COOK IT LONGER THAN INSTRUCTED, TAKING CARE NOT TO OVERCOOK TO THE POINT OF DRYNESS.

Salade Niçoise with Poached Salmon

SERVES 4

DRESSING

¼ cup lemon juice

2 teaspoons sugar

1½ tablespoons finely snipped fresh dill

¾ cup extra-virgin olive oil

SALAD

2 cups dry white wine

1 pound center-cut salmon fillet, cut
    crosswise into 4 equal portions

Salt

White pepper

¾ pound new potatoes

2 eggs

½ pound sugar snap peas, trimmed and
    stringed (see notes)

6 cups butter lettuce leaves

8 large leaves Belgian endive

2 Roma tomatoes

8 canned pickled whole red beets

¼ pound Niçoise olives, drained

Fresh dill sprigs, for garnish

1. First, make the dressing. In a small bowl, use a fork or small wire whisk to stir together the lemon juice and sugar until the sugar dissolves. Stir in the dill. Stirring briskly, pour in the oil in a thin, steady stream. Set aside.

2. Pour the wine into a nonreactive saucepan just big enough to hold the salmon fillets side by side. Bring the wine to a boil over medium-high heat; then reduce the heat to very low. Season the salmon fillets all over with salt and white pepper to taste and carefully place them in the pan. Cover and poach the salmon until the fillets are firm and completely opaque, checking by gently separating the flakes of one with the tip of a small, sharp knife. With a spatula, gently lift the fillets from the liquid and transfer them to a plate. Let them cool briefly, then cover with plastic wrap and refrigerate.

3. Put the potatoes in a saucepan with lightly salted cold water to cover. Bring to a boil over medium-high heat and cook potatoes until tender when pierced with the tip of a small, sharp knife, 10 to 15 minutes.

TEST KITCHEN NOTES

FRESH SALMON POACHED IN WHITE WINE AND THEN ALLOWED TO COOL MAKES A LOVELY VARIATION ON A CLASSIC. FOR THE BEST FLAVOR AND FEWEST BONES, ASK YOUR FISHMONGER TO CUT YOU THE FILLETS FROM THE CENTER OF A SIDE OF SALMON.

SMALL, FRESH SUGAR SNAP PEAS CAN BE EATEN RAW, BUT ARE GENERALLY AT THEIR BEST IF BRIEFLY PARBOILED, FOLLOWING THE RECIPE INSTRUCTIONS. BEFORE COOKING, TRIM AND STRING THE BEANS: WITH YOUR INDEX FINGER AND THUMB, SNAP THE STEM END OF EACH POD AND PULL ALONG THE STRAIGHT SEAM OF THE POD TO REMOVE THE FIBROUS STRINGS.

AN ALTERNATIVE TO SUGAR SNAP PEAS WOULD BE THE MORE COMMONLY AVAILABLE SNOW PEAS, ALSO KNOWN AS CHINESE PEA PODS OR MANGE-TOUT ("EAT-ALL," IN FRENCH). OR YOU COULD USE SLENDER STALKS OF ASPARAGUS.

THE SALMON, POTATOES, EGGS, AND SUGAR SNAPS MAY BE COOKED SEVERAL HOURS AHEAD OR THE NIGHT BEFORE AND REFRIGERATED.

At the same time, put the eggs in another saucepan of cold water and bring to a boil over medium-high heat. As soon as the water starts to boil, check the time and cook the eggs 10 minutes. Drain well, rinse with cold running water, and set the eggs aside.

Drain the potatoes. If the skins look unattractive, peel them off while the potatoes are still warm; otherwise, leave them on. Let the potatoes cool, then cut each one into 4 wedges. Put them in a small bowl and toss gently with just enough of the dressing to coat them. Set aside.

4. Meanwhile, bring yet another saucepan of salted water to a boil over medium-high heat. Add the sugar snap peas and parboil just 1 minute. Immediately drain them and rinse under cold running water until cool. Drain well and set aside.

5. Arrange the butter lettuce leaves in a bed on chilled individual serving plates. Place a salmon fillet across the center of each plate. Mound some of the potato salad next to the salmon fillet.

6. Peel the eggs and cut each lengthwise into quarters. Nestle a wedge of egg near each Belgian endive leaf and place 2 leaves and 2 wedges on each plate.

7. With a small, sharp knife, cut out the cores of the tomatoes. Cut the tomatoes lengthwise in quarters and arrange the tomato wedges on each plate.

8. Cut the beets into quarters. Arrange the peas and the beets on each plate.

9. Spoon more dressing liberally over the salmon, sugar snap peas, egg wedges, tomatoes, and beets. Garnish with the olives and fresh dill sprigs and serve immediately.

Chopped Salads

After much deliberation, I think I've finally figured out why chopped salads have become so popular: They remind us of nursery food, minced up into easy-to-eat pieces that, with every bite, whisk us back to happy childhood meals. Consider that the next time you see powerful business people ordering them for lunch.

Whether featuring cured meats or seafood, chopped salads seem to be the most popular of the genre. That doesn't mean, however, that the concept can't extend far and wide to other ingredients, as the recipes in this chapter demonstrate.

Whichever salads you plan to make, I recommend that you make a small investment in a large wooden chopping bowl and a *mezzaluna*, the Italian-style, half-moon-shaped chopper. Working with these two basic tools, you can put a chopped salad together in next to no time, and the work is extremely satisfying. Alternatively, you could prechop all the ingredients to the required size with a knife on a cutting board before tossing them with the dressing in a large salad bowl. The work will take a little bit longer, however, and you're not likely to have nearly as much fun.

Farmer's Style Vegetarian Chopped Salad

SERVES 4

DRESSING

¼ cup red wine vinegar
½ teaspoon salt
¼ teaspoon white pepper
¾ cup extra-virgin olive oil

SALAD

2 carrots, cut into ½-inch-thick slices
2 green bell peppers, quartered,
    stemmed, and seeded
2 stalks celery, cut into ½ inch-thick slices
1 cucumber, peeled, halved lengthwise,
    and seeded
8 red radishes, trimmed and
    thickly sliced
1 small red onion, coarsely chopped
¼ cup finely chopped Italian parsley
¼ cup finely shredded fresh basil leaves
14 ounces low-fat ricotta cheese, drained
¼ cup grated Parmesan cheese
1 head butter lettuce, leaves separated
Crostini (see page 19)
Fresh Italian parsley sprigs, for garnish

1. In a small mixing bowl, stir together the vinegar, salt, and pepper until the salt dissolves. Stirring continuously with a fork or small whisk, pour in the olive oil in a thin, steady stream, beating until emulsified. Set aside.

2. Put the carrots, peppers, celery, cucumber, radishes, and red onion in a large wooden chopping bowl. With a mezzaluna, chop into coarse pieces. Add the parsley, basil, ricotta, and Parmesan. Continue gently chopping and tossing the mixture until finely chopped into pieces about ¼ inch across. While tossing the mixture, add the dressing, thoroughly blending the salad.

3. Arrange the butter lettuce leaves to form beds on large, chilled, individual serving plates. Mound the salad in the center of each plate. Garnish with Crostini and parsley.

Neptune Chopped Salad

DRESSING

Thousand Island Dressing (see page 27)

SALAD

1 head iceberg lettuce, cored and
    quartered

1 head romaine, tough outer leaves
    discarded, remaining leaves cored,
    separated, and chilled

2 red bell peppers, quartered, stemmed,
    and seeded

1 cooked lobster tail (about ½ pound),
    shelled and cut into ½-inch-thick
    slices

½ pound cooked lump crabmeat, picked
    over to remove any gristle or shell

½ pound cooked bay shrimp

1 ripe but firm avocado, preferably
    Haas variety

2 tablespoons finely chopped fresh
    basil leaves

2 tablespoons finely chopped
    fresh chives

4 cups chicory leaves, coarsely torn

Lemon-Garlic Croutons (see page 18)

1. Prepare the dressing and set it aside.

2. Put the iceberg and romaine lettuce in a large wooden chopping bowl. With a mezzaluna, begin chopping them in the bowl until coarsely chopped. Add the bell peppers, lobster, crabmeat, and shrimp.

3. Quarter, pit, and peel the avocado and add it to the bowl. Continue chopping and tossing the mixture until it is chopped into pieces about ½ inch across. Add the basil and chives. While tossing the mixture with the mezzaluna, add just enough of the dressing to coat the salad well.

4. Arrange the chicory leaves around the edges of individual plates. Spoon the salad into the centers of the plates and garnish with the Lemon-Garlic Croutons.

TEST KITCHEN NOTES

I'VE LUNCHED ON NEPTUNE SALADS IN FABLED OLD CITY RESTAURANTS. BUT THOSE PRECURSORS—CONSISTING MAINLY OF ICEBERG LETTUCE AND SEAFOOD—ARE NOW AS DATED AS THE WOOD PANELING OF THOSE DINING ROOMS.

HERE, I'VE ADDED A FEW MORE INGREDIENTS TO BRING THE SALAD DECIDEDLY UP TO DATE. ROMAINE, MIXED WITH THE ICEBERG IN EQUAL PARTS, CONTRIBUTES A SLIGHTLY MORE ROBUST LETTUCE FLAVOR. RED BELL PEPPER ADDS BRIGHT COLOR, CRISPNESS, AND A SWEETNESS TO COMPLEMENT THAT OF THE SEAFOOD. AVOCADO ALSO COMPLEMENTS THEM WITH ITS RICH TASTE AND TEXTURE. FRESH HERBS ADD STILL MORE SPARK. AND THE CROUTONS BRING A MUCH-NEEDED CRUNCH.

IF YOU CAN'T GET THE THREE TYPES OF SHELLFISH CALLED FOR, JUST PURCHASE EXTRA QUANTITIES OF THOSE THAT ARE AVAILABLE; DON'T LET THE SHORTAGE OF A LOBSTER TAIL, FOR EXAMPLE, DEPRIVE YOU OF A CLASSIC CHOPPED SALAD EXPERIENCE.

Traditional Italian Chopped Salad with Red Kidney Beans and Soppressata

SERVES 4

DRESSING

¼ cup balsamic vinegar

½ teaspoon salt

¼ teaspoon black pepper

¾ cup extra-virgin olive oil

SALAD

2 large heads romaine, tough outer leaves discarded, remaining leaves cored and separated

6 ounces sliced soppressata or other Italian-style cured salami

6 ounces sliced provolone cheese

1 can (about 15 ounces) red kidney beans, rinsed and drained

2 red bell peppers, roasted, peeled, stemmed, and seeded (see pages 15–16), torn into long strips, juices reserved

¼ cup finely chopped fresh chives

¼ cup finely chopped Italian parsley

¼ cup pine nuts, toasted (see page 17)

1 dozen Italian-style cured black olives

1. First, make the dressing. In a small mixing bowl, stir together the balsamic vinegar, salt, and black pepper until the salt dissolves. Stirring continuously with a fork or small whisk, pour in the olive oil in a thin, steady stream, beating until emulsified. Set aside.

2. Put the romaine leaves in a large wooden chopping bowl. With a mezzaluna, begin chopping them in the bowl until coarsely chopped. Add the soppressata, provolone, red beans, roasted peppers, chives, and parsley and continue chopping and tossing the mixture until finely chopped into pieces about ¼ inch across. Still tossing the mixture, add the dressing and the pine nuts.

3. Spoon the salad into individual shallow pasta-serving bowls. Garnish with olives.

TEST KITCHEN NOTES

YOU DON'T NEED TO HAVE A GOOD ITALIAN DELICATESSEN NEARBY TO SHOP FOR THE INGREDIENTS, BUT IT HELPS. SOPPRESSATA IS A HIGHLY FLAVORFUL TYPE OF ITALIAN CURED PORK SALAMI. YOU COULD SUBSTITUTE ITALIAN SALAMI OR GOOD IMPORTED ITALIAN PROSCIUTTO. WHICHEVER TYPE OF CURED MEAT YOU USE, MAKE SURE TO BUY IT THINLY SLICED, WHICH WILL HELP YOU CHOP IT UP.

THE SAME SLICING INSTRUCTIONS GO FOR THE PROVOLONE CHEESE. YOU COULD ALSO SUBSTITUTE MOZZARELLA (PREFERABLY FRESH), THOUGH IT DOESN'T SLICE AS NEATLY.

IF YOU'RE PRESSED FOR TIME, PICK UP A JAR OF ROASTED RED PEPPERS. PACKED IN OIL OR VINEGAR, USUALLY WITH SUGAR AND SPICES, THEY'LL MAKE A VERY TASTY SUBSTITUTE FOR THE HOME-ROASTED PEPPERS CALLED FOR.

Tuna and White Bean Chopped Salad

SERVES 4

DRESSING

¼ cup fresh lemon juice

1 teaspoon sugar

½ teaspoon salt

¼ teaspoon white pepper

¾ cup extra-virgin olive oil

SALAD

2 large heads radicchio, leaves separated

2 large heads romaine, tough outer
leaves discarded, remaining leaves
cored, separated, and chilled

1 red bell pepper, quartered, stemmed,
and seeded

2 cans (about 6 ounces each) Italian-style
tuna in olive oil, drained

2 cans (about 15 ounces each) Italian
cannellini (white kidney) beans,
rinsed well and drained

2 tablespoons finely chopped
fresh chives

2 tablespoons finely snipped fresh dill

2 tablespoons finely chopped
Italian parsley

2 large shallots, coarsely chopped

4 small sprigs fresh chervil, dill, or Italian
parsley, for garnish

1. In a small mixing bowl, stir together the lemon juice, sugar, salt, and white pepper until the sugar and salt dissolve. Stirring continuously with a fork or small whisk, pour in the olive oil in a thin, steady stream, beating until emulsified. Set aside.

2. Cut the radicchio leaves into long strips and evenly distribute the strips among the serving plates.

3. Put the romaine leaves and red bell pepper quarters in a large wooden chopping bowl. With a mezzaluna, begin chopping them in the bowl until coarsely chopped. Add the tuna, cannellini beans, chives, dill, and parsley and continue chopping and tossing the mixture until finely chopped into pieces about ¼ inch across. Add the shallots. While tossing the mixture, add just enough of the dressing to coat the salad well.

4. Spoon the salad onto the beds of sliced radicchio leaves. Garnish with chervil, dill, or parsley sprigs.

TEST KITCHEN NOTES

TONNO E FAGIOLI, A TRADITIONAL ITALIAN APPETIZER OF CANNED TUNA TOSSED WITH CANNELLINI (WHITE KIDNEY) BEANS, WAS THE INSPIRATION FOR THIS CHOPPED SALAD. FOR THE MOST AUTHENTIC TASTE, I RECOMMEND THAT YOU USE IMPORTED ITALIAN TUNA PACKED IN OLIVE OIL, ALTHOUGH YOU COULD, IF YOU WISH, MAKE IT WITH DOMESTIC WATER-PACKED TUNA AND STILL GET GOOD RESULTS.

JUST A HINT OF PROSCIUTTO—SAY, 2 OR 3 OUNCES FOR FOUR SALADS—ADDS A SUBTLE EDGE OF SALTY RICHNESS TO THE SALAD, A NICE COMPLEMENT TO THE TUNA. ANOTHER OPTION WOULD BE TO INCLUDE A FEW ANCHOVY FILLETS.

LARGE OUTER LEAVES FROM A HEAD OF RADICCHIO MAKE A NICELY CONTRASTING BED ON WHICH TO PRESENT THE SALAD. IF YOU CAN'T FIND RADICCHIO, USE ANY LETTUCES THAT COME TO HAND—PERHAPS THE OUTER LEAVES YOU'D OTHERWISE DISCARD FROM THE ROMAINE.

Spring Chicken Chopped Salad with Herbed Lemon Cream Dressing

SERVES 4

CHICKEN AND SPRING VEGETABLES

4 cups chicken broth

2 medium-size carrots, cut crosswise into ½-inch-thick slices

2 dozen asparagus spears, trimmed

1 pound boneless, skinless chicken breasts

DRESSING

¼ cup lemon juice

¾ teaspoon sugar

¾ teaspoon salt

¼ teaspoon white pepper

1 cup heavy cream, chilled

2 tablespoons finely chopped fresh basil

2 tablespoons finely chopped fresh chives

2 tablespoons finely snipped fresh dill

SALAD

2 red bell peppers, quartered, stemmed, and seeded

2 shallots, coarsely chopped

1 medium-size cucumber, peeled, halved lengthwise, and seeded

6 cups mixed baby salad leaves

1. First, prepare the chicken and vegetables. In a wide saucepan, bring the broth to a boil over medium-high heat. Add the carrots and asparagus and simmer until crisp-tender, about 3 minutes. Remove the vegetables with a slotted spoon and set aside in a bowl to cool, then cover and chill in the refrigerator.

2. Put the chicken in the still-simmering broth, cover, and cook, turning the chicken occasionally, until it is cooked through, 7 to 10 minutes. Remove the chicken from the broth with a slotted spoon and let cool, then cover and chill in the refrigerator.

3. Before assembling the salad, make the dressing. In a mixing bowl, use a wire whisk to stir together the lemon juice, sugar, salt, and pepper until the salt dissolves. Whisking continuously, slowly pour in the cream, continuing to whisk until the mixture is thick but still fluid. Stir in the herbs.

4. With a sharp knife, cut off the tips of the asparagus spears and reserve them. In a large wooden chopping bowl, put the remaining asparagus stalks along with the carrots, bell peppers, shallots, and cucumber. With your fingers, tear the cooked chicken into chunks and add them to the bowl.

Using a mezzaluna, chop the ingredients, turning and tossing the mixture until you have pieces about ¼ to ½ inch across. Pour in enough of the dressing to coat the pieces evenly to your liking, using the mezzaluna to toss the mixture.

5. Arrange beds of mixed baby greens on individual plates and mound the chopped salad on top. Garnish with the asparagus tips.

TEST KITCHEN NOTES

IF ONE CHOPPED SALAD ALONE HAS THE POWER TO SUMMON THE ESSENCE OF SPRINGTIME, THIS IS IT—TENDER-CRISP VEGETABLES, A BOUQUET OF FRESH HERBS, AND CHUNKS OF POACHED CHICKEN BREAST, ALL ENVELOPED IN A CREAMY, TANGY DRESSING.

YOU COULD MAKE THE SALAD, IF YOU WISH, WITH LEFTOVER CHICKEN, WHITE MEAT OR DARK, FROM THE PREVIOUS EVENING'S ROAST. I FIND, HOWEVER, THAT IT TASTES ALL THE BETTER AND MORE SUCCULENT WHEN YOU FRESHLY POACH THE CHICKEN BREASTS AN HOUR OR TWO BEFORE SERVING TIME.

Diner-style Chopped Chef's Salad

SERVES 4

DRESSING

Classic Blue Cheese or Ranch Dressing
(see pages 25 and 26)

SALAD

2 medium-size heads iceberg lettuce,
12 outer leaves reserved, remaining
leaves cored and quartered

1 small red onion, peeled and quartered

¼ pound thinly sliced roast turkey breast

¼ pound thinly sliced roast beef

¼ pound thinly sliced baked ham

¼ pound thinly sliced sharp
Cheddar cheese

¼ pound thinly sliced Swiss cheese

¼ cup finely chopped Italian parsley

4 Roma tomatoes, cored and cut into
thin wedges

1. Prepare the dressing and set it aside.

2. Put the iceberg lettuce wedges and red onion quarters in a large wooden chopping bowl. With a mezzaluna, begin chopping them in the bowl until coarsely chopped. Add the turkey, beef, ham, Cheddar and Swiss cheeses, and parsley, and continue chopping and tossing the mixture until finely chopped into pieces about ¼ inch across. Still tossing with the mezzaluna, add enough of the dressing to coat the salad well.

3. Arrange the reserved iceberg leaves to form bowl shapes on individual serving plates. Mound the salad in the center. Garnish with tomato wedges.

TEST KITCHEN NOTES

I HAVE LONG FOUND THE CLASSIC CHEF'S SALAD TO BE DISCONCERTING IN ITS PRESENTATION. WITH ALL THE FEATURED INGREDIENTS CUT INTO BIG STRIPS AND LAID OUT IN NEAT SECTIONS ATOP THE LETTUCE, I WOULD BE REDUCED TO COMPOSING INDIVIDUAL BITES ON MY FORK BY FIRST SPEARING A SINGLE STRIP OF TURKEY, THEN BEEF, THEN HAM, SUPPLEMENTING THEM WITH A LITTLE CHEESE, AND THEN FINALLY SPEARING A CHUNK OF LETTUCE. NEXT CAME THE STRUGGLE TO GET THE WHOLE THING INTO MY MOUTH. THE SOLUTION TO THIS DILEMMA, OF COURSE, WAS TO CHOP ALL THE INGREDIENTS TOGETHER.

HERE, I'VE ADDED JUST A HINT OF SWEET RED ONION, A MUCH BETTER WAY TO ENJOY ITS FLAVOR THAN THE UNWIELDY RINGS OF ONION SOME CHEFS USE AS A GARNISH. YOU COULD JUST AS WELL CHOP INTO THE SALAD SOME RAW OR ROASTED BELL PEPPER.

I'VE ALWAYS PREFERRED MY CHEF'S SALADS WITH A CREAMY DRESSING LIKE BLUE CHEESE OR RANCH, WHICH I CALL FOR HERE. OF COURSE, YOU COULD DRESS THE SALAD WITH A VINAIGRETTE, OR GO WHOLE HOG ON THE DINER ROUTE AND USE YOUR FAVORITE BRAND OF BOTTLED THOUSAND ISLAND OR FRENCH DRESSING.

Deli-style Chopped Chef's Salad

SERVES 4

DRESSING

Russian Dressing (see page 27)

SALAD

1 medium-size head red cabbage, cored,
    6 outer leaves reserved, remaining
    leaves quartered and cut crosswise
    into thin slices

1 medium-size head iceberg lettuce,
    6 outer leaves reserved, remaining
    leaves cored and quartered

1 sweet yellow onion, such as Vidalia,
    peeled and quartered

2 large dill pickles, drained well and cut
    lengthwise into spears

½ pound thinly sliced lean corned beef

½ pound thinly sliced pastrami

½ pound thinly sliced Swiss cheese

2 medium-size carrots, shredded

¼ cup finely chopped Italian parsley

4 Roma tomatoes, cored and cut into
    thin wedges

Toasted bagel chips

1. Prepare the dressing and set it aside.

2. Bring a kettle of water to a boil. Separate the red cabbage into shreds and arrange them in a strainer or colander. Pour the boiling water from the kettle evenly over the shreds to wilt them all. Rinse with cold running water and drain.

3. Put the cabbage, iceberg lettuce wedges, onion quarters, and dill pickle spears in a large wooden chopping bowl. With a mezzaluna, coarsely chop. Add the corned beef, pastrami, and Swiss cheese, and continue chopping and tossing the mixture until finely chopped into pieces about ¼ inch across. Add the carrots and parsley. Still tossing with the mezzaluna, add enough of the dressing to coat the salad well.

4. Arrange the reserved red cabbage and iceberg leaves to form bowl shapes on individual serving plates. Mound the salad in the center. Garnish with tomato wedges and toasted bagel chips.

Chili Beef Chopped Taco Salad

SERVES 4

DRESSING

Ranch Dressing (see page 26)

SALAD

2 tablespoons olive oil
1 onion, finely chopped
1 tablespoon chili powder
1 pound extra-lean ground beef
2 medium-size heads iceberg lettuce,
    cored and cut into quarters
2 cans (about 15 ounces each) kidney
    beans, rinsed and drained
2 ripe but firm avocados
6 ounces Cheddar cheese, thinly sliced
¼ cup finely chopped fresh
    cilantro leaves
8 ounces tortilla or corn chips
½ cup fresh tomato salsa
Fresh cilantro sprigs, for garnish

1. First, make the dressing and set it aside.

2. In a heavy skillet, heat the olive oil over medium heat. Add the onion and sauté, stirring frequently with a wooden spoon, for about 1 minute. Sprinkle in the chili powder and sauté, stirring continuously, until it is fragrant, about 30 seconds more. Add the ground beef and continue sautéing, stirring frequently to break up the meat into coarse chunks, until it is evenly browned, about 5 minutes more. Set the beef aside.

3. Put the iceberg lettuce wedges in a large wooden chopping bowl. With a mezzaluna, begin chopping them in the bowl until coarsely chopped. Add the cooked beef and kidney beans.

4. Quarter, pit, and peel the avocados and add them to the bowl along with the cheese and cilantro. Continue chopping and tossing the mixture until finely chopped into pieces about ¼ inch across.

5. With your hands, coarsely crush in about three-fourths of the tortilla or corn chips, reserving the rest for a garnish. Still tossing with the mezzaluna, add the dressing to coat the salad well.

6. Mound the salad onto large, chilled, individual serving plates or bowls. Arrange the remaining chips around the edges of the salad. Spoon large dollops of the salsa on top of each salad and garnish with cilantro sprigs.

Scandinavian Chopped Herring Salad with Beet, Potato, Apple, Onion, and Cucumber

SERVES 4

DRESSING

¼ cup cider vinegar

½ teaspoon sugar

¼ teaspoon salt

¼ teaspoon white pepper

¾ cup vegetable oil

SALAD

2 medium-size boiling potatoes

2 green apples

1 small red onion, quartered

12 small sweet pickled gherkins, drained well

12 small canned pickled beets

2 jars (6 ounces each) bottled pickled herring fillets in wine

2 tablespoons coarsely snipped fresh dill

1 head butter lettuce

Fresh dill sprigs, for garnish

1. In a small mixing bowl, stir together the vinegar, sugar, salt, and pepper until the sugar and salt dissolve. Stirring continuously with a fork or small whisk, pour in the vegetable oil in a thin, steady stream. Set aside.

2. Put the potatoes in a small saucepan of water and bring to a boil over medium-high heat. Boil until the potatoes are tender when pierced with the tip of a small, sharp knife, 15 to 20 minutes. Drain well. While still hot, carefully peel the potatoes and cut them into quarters. Set aside.

3. Quarter and core the apples and put them in a large wooden chopping bowl with the red onion and gherkins. With a mezzaluna, begin chopping them in the bowl until coarsely chopped. Add the potatoes, beets, herring pieces, and dill, and continue gently chopping and tossing the mixture until finely chopped into pieces about ¼ inch across. Still tossing the mixture with the mezzaluna, add the dressing to coat the salad well. Transfer to a nonreactive glass or ceramic bowl, cover, and chill in the refrigerator for at least 1 hour.

4. Arrange the butter lettuce leaves to form beds on individual serving plates. Mound the salad in the center of each plate. Garnish with dill sprigs.

TEST KITCHEN NOTES

PICKLED HERRING IS A REFINED, GROWN-UP TASTE, BUT NOTHING ELSE OFFERS QUITE THE SAME COMBINATION OF HEADY OCEAN FLAVOR, BRACING TANG, AND SATISFYING MEATINESS.

HERRING ON ITS OWN CAN BE PRETTY POWERFUL, TO BE TAKEN IN MEASURED DOSES. THAT IS WHY I LIKE THIS SCANDINAVIAN-INSPIRED SALAD SO MUCH, PARTNERING THE HERRING AS IT DOES WITH SEVERAL COMPLEMENTARY INGREDIENTS—POTATOES, APPLES, ONION, PICKLED CUCUMBERS, AND PICKLED BEETS.

OFFER THIS DELICIOUS, PUNGENT SALAD AS A SPECIAL LUNCHEON FOR HERRING-LOVING FRIENDS. SERVE WITH A LOAF OF GOOD, FRESHLY BAKED BLACK BREAD OR RYE BREAD, CUT INTO ULTRA-THIN SLICES IN THE SCANDINAVIAN STYLE; SOME SOFTENED, UNSALTED BUTTER; AND VERY WELL-CHILLED BEER OR SHOTS OF ICED AQUAVIT—BOTH OF WHICH HAVE THE ABILITY TO CLEANSE AND REFRESH THE PALATE AFTER EVERY SINGLE BITE.

Chopped Tropical Ambrosia with Coconut Cream Dressing

SERVES 4

1 ripe pineapple

1 ripe mango

1 ripe papaya

4 navel oranges

1 small or ½ large jícama (about 6 ounces total), peeled and cut into ½ inch-thick slices

2 tablespoons lime juice

1 cup macadamia nuts, toasted (see page 17)

1 cup canned coconut cream

2 tablespoons finely chopped fresh mint leaves

1 dozen whole romaine leaves

1 ripe kiwi fruit, peeled and cut into ¼-inch-thick slices

Fresh mint sprigs, for garnish

1. With a large, sharp knife, cut off the top and bottom of the pineapple. Stand the pineapple upright and, slicing downward, peel away its skin in thick strips. With the tip of a small, sharp knife, cut out any remaining tough "eyes" from the fruit. With the pineapple still upright, cut downward to slice the fruit away from the thick, woody central core; discard the core.

2. With a small, sharp knife, peel the mango. Then, cut the fruit away from the large, flat central stone in thick slices. Set aside with the pineapple.

3. Halve, peel, and seed the papaya and cut it lengthwise into ½-inch-thick slices. Set them aside with the mango and pineapple.

4. With a sharp knife, cut off the stem and navel ends of the oranges in slices thick enough to reveal the fruit. One at a time, stand the oranges on their navel ends and cut off the peel in strips thick enough to remove the membranes and reveal the fruit. Holding each orange in your hand over a mixing bowl, use a small, sharp knife to cut between the fruit and membrane of each segment, allowing it to drop into the bowl.

5. Put the jícama slices in a large wooden chopping bowl. With a mezzaluna, chop them into pieces about 1 inch across. Add the lime juice and toss gently to coat the jícama.

6. Add the pineapple, mango, papaya, and orange segments, and continue chopping until you have pieces about ½ inch in size.

Add the macadamia nuts, coconut cream, and chopped mint leaves and, with the mezzaluna, gently fold the mixture together. Transfer to a bowl, cover, and chill in the refrigerator for at least 1 hour.

7. Arrange the romaine leaves on individual serving plates. Mound the salad in the center and garnish with kiwi slices and mint sprigs.

CHAPTER 5

Robust Salads

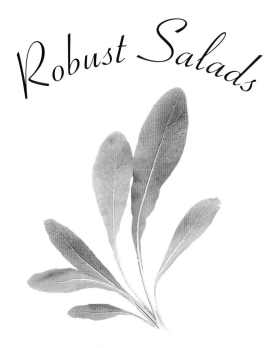

This chapter is about salads abounding with grilled steak, fried chicken, or sizzling sausage; salads that dazzle the taste buds with exotic Asian spices or such intense flavors as sharp, creamy goat cheese, mustardy fruits, or hot and spicy peanut dressing; salads that offer the comfort of *al dente* pasta or boiled potatoes—salads, in short, that satisfy.

The concept of robust salads might at first seem to fly in the face of convention. In general, one expects a salad to be light. But all the above-mentioned suggestions offer convincing solutions to the conundrum. Through judicious measures of meaty or other rich elements, through seasonings that satiate the senses, and through favorite ingredients guaranteed to fill you up, a salad can be robust even as it also retains its characteristic lightness, leaving you feeling pleasantly refreshed, as a good salad should.

BUFFALO CHICKEN SALAD

BBLT SALAD

GERMAN POTATO SALAD WITH
GRILLED SAUSAGE AND WHOLE-
GRAIN MUSTARD DRESSING

INDONESIAN CHICKEN SALAD WITH
HOT AND SPICY PEANUT DRESSING

CHINESE STREET MARKET CHICKEN
CHOW MEIN SALAD

ITALIAN STEAK SALAD WITH
ARUGULA, GORGONZOLA, AND
BALSAMIC VINAIGRETTE

OVEN-FRIED CHICKEN ON PICKLED
VEGETABLE SLAW WITH BACON AND
PECANS

GREEK COUNTRY-STYLE
LAMB SALAD

MOROCCAN GRILLED LAMB SALAD
WITH COUSCOUS AND DRIED FRUIT

GRILLED CURRIED CHICKEN SALAD

SAUTÉED MUSHROOM SALAD
WITH GOAT CHEESE AND
SUN-DRIED TOMATOES

BRUSCHETTA TOMATO SALAD WITH
PROSCIUTTO AND MOZZARELLA

SPINACH AND GOAT CHEESE SALAD
WITH DRIED FRUIT AND WARM
HONEY-MUSTARD VINAIGRETTE

GRILLED PORK AND
FRESH FIG SALAD

THE BAKED POTATO SALAD

GRILLED VEGETABLE SALAD WITH
GOAT CHEESE AND PINE NUTS

Buffalo Chicken Salad

SERVES 4

DRESSING

1 cup Ranch Dressing (see page 26)

SALAD

4 boneless, skinless chicken breast halves
(4 to 6 ounces each)

¾ cup spicy barbecue sauce

1 large red onion, cut into
½-inch-thick slices

2 tablespoons unsalted butter, melted

Salt

Black pepper

2 heads romaine, cored and torn into
bite-size pieces (about 14 cups total)

4 stalks celery, cut crosswise into
¼-inch slices

2 dozen canned pitted black olives,
cut in half

Garlic Toasts (see page 19)

¼ cup finely chopped Italian parsley

1. Make the dressing and set aside.

2. Preheat the broiler or grill.

3. Meanwhile, put the chicken breasts in a bowl and pour ½ cup of the barbecue sauce over them; reserve the remaining sauce for serving. Turn the chicken well to coat evenly and leave to marinate about 15 minutes.

4. Brush the onion slices with the melted butter and season them well with salt and pepper. Leaving the chicken breasts thickly coated with the sauce, season with salt and pepper and arrange them and the onion slices on the broiler or grill rack. Cook until both the chicken and onions are cooked through and well browned, about 5 minutes per side.

5. While the chicken and onions are cooking, prepare the salad. Put the lettuce in a large mixing bowl and toss well with the dressing. Arrange the lettuce in beds on large, chilled, individual serving plates.

6. When the chicken and onions are done, separate the onions into rings and strew them on top of the lettuce. Cut each chicken breast crosswise into slices ¼ to ½ inch wide and arrange the slices on each salad. Drizzle the remaining barbecue sauce over the chicken. Scatter the celery and black olives on top and tuck the Garlic Toasts around the sides of each salad. Garnish with parsley and serve immediately.

TEST KITCHEN NOTES

I'VE NEVER PARTICULARLY LIKED BUFFALO-STYLE CHICKEN WINGS, SIMPLY BECAUSE I DON'T PARTICULARLY ENJOY CHICKEN WINGS IN ANY FORM. BUT I CAN UNDERSTAND THE DISH'S WIDESPREAD APPEAL: THE CONTRAST OF TENDER CHICKEN MEAT AND THE CRISP CELERY THAT ACCOMPANIES IT; THE HOT TANG OF THE CHICKEN'S SAUCE PLAYING OFF THE COOL CREAMINESS OF THE CELERY'S DIP; THE DIVINE MESSINESS OF THE WHOLE CONCEPT!

THOSE TEMPTING ASPECTS OF THE POPULAR APPETIZER INSPIRED ME TO MAKE A SALAD VERSION THAT I COULD—AND DO—THOROUGHLY ENJOY. THE WINGS ARE REPLACED BY BONELESS, SKINLESS CHICKEN BREASTS, WHICH ARE FAR EASIER TO EAT IN A SALAD AND MUCH HEALTHIER AS WELL. THE CELERY IS THINLY SLICED AND USED AS A CRUNCHY TOPPING. A BED OF CRISP ROMAINE SEEMED TO ME TO BE THE PERFECT BASE FOR THE WHOLE CONSTRUCTION. TO ROUND THINGS OUT, I'VE ALSO ADDED GRILLED RED ONION, WHICH GOES SO WELL WITH BARBECUED CHICKEN, A FEW PITTED BLACK OLIVES, AND SOME CRISP GARLIC TOASTS.

BBLT Salad

DRESSING

1 cup Ranch Dressing (see page 26)
1½ tablespoons prepared white
   horseradish

SALAD

½ pound smoked bacon, thinly sliced
2 medium-size heads romaine, cored,
   leaves separated and torn into
   bite-size pieces
¾ pound roast beef, thinly sliced
2 dozen cherry tomatoes, stemmed and
   cut in half
¼ cup coarsely chopped Italian parsley

1. To make the dressing, put the Ranch Dressing in a mixing bowl and stir in the horseradish. Set aside.

2. Before assembling the salad, cook the bacon. Arrange the strips side by side in one or two frying pans and cook over medium heat, turning frequently, until crisp and brown, about 10 minutes. Remove the bacon and set aside to drain on several layers of paper toweling.

3. To assemble the salad, arrange the lettuce in beds on large individual serving plates. Drape the slices of roast beef evenly on top of the lettuce. Arrange the cherry tomatoes on top of the beef. Crumble the bacon over the salads and garnish with parsley. Pass the dressing on the side or drizzle it over each salad.

TEST KITCHEN NOTES

HOW TO TRANSLATE THE APPEAL OF A BACON, LETTUCE, AND TOMATO SANDWICH INTO A SALAD—THAT'S THE CHALLENGE I POSED TO MYSELF WHEN STARTING TO DEVELOP THIS RECIPE. BUT SOMETHING WAS NEEDED TO TRANSFORM THIS FAVORITE INTO A TRULY ROBUST SALAD.

THAT MISSING INGREDIENT, FOR ME, WAS ROAST BEEF (THE EXTRA "B" OF THE TITLE), WHICH GOES SO WELL WITH ALL THE OTHER ELEMENTS. THE SOURCE FOR THE BEEF COULD BE LAST NIGHT'S ROAST, OR YOU COULD BUY IT SLICED TO ORDER FROM THE DELICATESSEN.

CHERRY TOMATOES, I FOUND, LOOK VERY PRETTY ON THE SALAD. YOU COULD SUBSTITUTE REGULAR TOMATOES, OR INCLUDE SOME GOLDEN CHERRY OR TEARDROP-SHAPED TOMATOES.

THE FINISHING TOUCH COMES WITH ADDING A LITTLE PREPARED HORSERADISH TO A TRADITIONAL RANCH DRESSING. THERE'S NOT ENOUGH OF THE FIERY ROOT HERE TO MAKE YOUR EYES WATER, THOUGH; I'VE INCLUDED JUST ENOUGH TO MAKE YOU STOP AND TAKE NOTICE OF THE INTERESTING TASTE IT CONTRIBUTES.

ACCOMPANY THE SALAD WITH SOME SORT OF TOASTED BREAD, SUCH AS PARMESAN TOASTS (SEE PAGE 19), OR JUST HUNKS OF A HOT, CRUSTY LOAF.

German Potato Salad with Grilled Sausage and Whole-Grain Mustard Dressing

SERVES 4

DRESSING

3 tablespoons apple cider vinegar

½ teaspoon sugar

¼ teaspoon salt

¼ teaspoon white pepper

1 heaping tablespoon whole-grain
    German-style or grainy
    Dijon mustard

2 tablespoons finely chopped
    fresh chives

½ cup vegetable oil

SALAD

2 pounds Yukon Gold or other waxy
    yellow potatoes

4 German-style weisswurst or bratwurst
    (4 to 6 ounces each)

3 cups small spinach leaves,
    thoroughly washed, stemmed,
    and coarsely torn

3 cups radicchio leaves, coarsely torn

12 whole chives, for garnish

1. Preheat the broiler.

2. First, make the dressing. In a bowl large enough to hold the potatoes, use a fork or small wire whisk to stir together the vinegar, sugar, salt, and white pepper until the sugar and salt dissolve. Add the mustard and stir until blended. Stir in the chives. Stirring continuously, pour in the oil in a thin, steady stream.

3. Put the potatoes in a large saucepan with lightly salted cold water to cover. Bring to a boil over medium-high heat; boil until tender enough to be pierced with the tip of a small, sharp knife, 15 to 20 minutes.

4. At the same time you start the potatoes, puncture each weisswurst in several places with a fork and put the sausages in a saucepan with cold water to cover. Bring to a boil over medium-high heat. As soon as the water reaches a full rolling boil, drain well.

5. As soon as the potatoes are done, drain them well. One at a time, hold the hot potatoes in a folded kitchen towel to protect your hand and, with a small, sharp knife, cut them into slices about ½ inch thick, letting the slices fall into the bowl of dressing. Use wooden spoons to toss the potatoes gently and let them stand at room temperature until tepid.

6. Put the drained sausages on the broiler tray and broil them until evenly browned, 3 to 4 minutes per side.

7. While the sausages broil, toss together the spinach and radicchio, and arrange the leaves in beds on large individual serving plates. Mound the potato salad on top of the bed of leaves.

8. When the sausages are done, cut each one crosswise on the diagonal into slices about ½ inch thick. Arrange the slices on top of the potatoes, garnish with chives, and serve immediately.

TEST KITCHEN NOTES

THE DISH KNOWN AS GERMAN POTATO SALAD—WARM POTATOES TOSSED WITH A DRESSING WHICH THEY SOAK UP AS THEY COOL—IS A FREQUENT ACCOMPANIMENT TO GRILLED FRESH SAUSAGES. I'VE TAKEN THE LIBERTY OF SLICING THE SAUSAGE AND OF ADDING THE MUSTARD THAT IS USUALLY DABBED ON EACH BITE OF SAUSAGE TO THE POTATO SALAD'S DRESSING.

Indonesian Chicken Salad with Hot and Spicy Peanut Dressing

SERVES 4

DRESSING

1½ tablespoons vegetable oil

4 red or green serrano chili peppers
    or 1 jalapeño

1-inch piece fresh ginger

1 medium-size shallot

1 teaspoon anchovy paste

1 cup chunky-style peanut butter

¾ cup water

½ cup canned coconut milk

2 tablespoons honey

1½ tablespoons seasoned rice vinegar

1½ tablespoons soy sauce

SALAD

1¾ cups chicken broth

1 tablespoon soy sauce

4 thin slices fresh ginger

½ pound snow peas, trimmed

½ pound bean sprouts

2 medium-size carrots, thinly sliced

¾ pound chicken tenders or boneless,
    skinless chicken breasts

2 heads napa cabbage

2 red bell peppers, halved, stemmed,
    seeded, and cut lengthwise into
    thin strips

1 bag (about 2 ounces) shrimp chips

2 tablespoons finely chopped fresh
    cilantro

1. Prepare the vegetables and chicken at least 2 hours and up to 24 hours before serving time. Put the chicken broth, soy sauce, and ginger slices in a medium-size saucepan and bring to a boil over medium-high heat. Add the snow peas and parboil until crisp-tender, about 2 minutes, removing them with a slotted spoon and transferring them to a bowl. Do the same with the bean sprouts, cooking them for about 30 seconds; then the carrot slices, cooking them for about 2 minutes.

2. Reduce the heat under the pan of broth to very low, add the chicken, cover, and poach until cooked through, about 10 minutes for tenders, 15 minutes for breast halves. Let the chicken cool in the broth at room temperature about 30 minutes, then transfer the chicken and broth to the bowl with the vegetables, cover with plastic wrap, and refrigerate until cold.

3. To assemble the salads, cut the heads of napa cabbage crosswise into ¼-inch-wide strips, discarding the core of each head. On large individual serving plates, arrange the cabbage, snow peas, bean sprouts, and carrots in attractive beds. Cut the chicken crosswise into ¼- to ½-inch pieces and arrange them on top with slices of red pepper.

4. To make the dressing, put the oil in a medium-size saucepan. With the fine holes of a grater, grate the chilies, ginger, and shallot directly into the pan and add the anchovy paste. Put the pan over medium-low heat and stir the mixture with a wooden spoon to combine the ingredients into a smooth paste. As soon as the paste begins to sizzle, add the peanut butter, water, coconut milk, honey, rice vinegar, and soy sauce. Continue stirring the mixture until it is heated through, adding a little more water if necessary to give it a thick but fluid consistency.

5. Spoon the hot dressing generously over each salad. Garnish the salads with shrimp chips and cilantro and serve immediately.

TEST KITCHEN NOTES

THIS IS A VERSION OF *GADO GADO*, INDONESIA'S TRADITIONAL AND SPECTACULAR VEGETABLE SALAD, IN WHICH ALL MANNER OF COLD, RAW, OR PARBOILED VEGETABLES ARE TOSSED WITH A SIMMERED, SPICED DRESSING BASED ON PEANUT BUTTER. TRADITIONAL RECIPES CALL FOR THE ADDITION OF HARD-TO-FIND *NAM PLA*, A PUNGENT-SMELLING PASTE OF FERMENTED FISH. I USED ANCHOVY PASTE INSTEAD.

Chinese Street Market Chicken Chow Mein Salad

SERVES 4

SALAD

1¾ cups chicken broth

1 tablespoon soy sauce

4 thin slices fresh ginger

¾ pound boneless, skinless chicken meat

8 ounces dried chow mein or Japanese *chuka soba* noodles

½ pound bean sprouts

4 green onions, thinly sliced

1 cucumber, coarsely shredded

1 large carrot, coarsely shredded

3 tablespoons finely chopped fresh cilantro

4 cups spinach leaves, thoroughly washed

Fresh cilantro sprigs, for garnish

DRESSING

¾ cup sesame paste (*tahini*)

3 tablespoons seasoned rice vinegar

1 tablespoon soy sauce

1 tablespoon finely grated fresh ginger

1 tablespoon sugar

4 to 6 tablespoons hot water

1. If making the chicken fresh for this salad, prepare it at least 2 hours and up to 24 hours before serving time. Put the chicken broth, soy sauce, and ginger slices in a medium-size saucepan and bring to a boil over medium-high heat. Reduce the heat to very low, add the chicken, cover, and poach until cooked through, 10 to 15 minutes. Let the chicken cool in the broth at room temperature for about 30 minutes, then transfer the chicken and broth to a bowl, cover with plastic wrap, and refrigerate until cold.

2. To prepare the salad, bring a large saucepan of water to a boil over medium-high heat. Add the chow mein noodles and boil until tender but still chewy, about 3 minutes or according to the package directions.

3. Put the bean sprouts in the strainer you will use to drain the noodles. Pour the pot of noodles over the bean sprouts to drain, wilting the bean sprouts in the process. Rinse well under cold running water to cool the noodles and sprouts, then drain well.

Transfer the noodles and sprouts to a large mixing bowl. Add the green onions, cucumber, carrot, and cilantro. Tear the chicken into thin, bite-size shreds and add it to the bowl, reserving the broth for another use, if you wish. Toss the ingredients lightly to combine them.

4. Prepare the dressing. In a small mixing bowl, stir together the sesame paste, rice vinegar, soy sauce, ginger, and sugar; they will form a fairly thick paste. Little by little, stir in enough of the hot water to thin the paste to a smooth, creamy, fluid consistency.

Pour the dressing over the salad mixture and toss well to coat all the ingredients.

5. Arrange the spinach leaves to form beds on large individual serving plates or bowls. Mound the salad on top of the spinach and garnish with cilantro sprigs.

TEST KITCHEN NOTES

A WHILE BACK, NOODLE MIXTURES LIKE THIS—CALLED *DAN DAN MEIN* OR SOME PHONETIC VARIATION ON THAT—WERE ALL THE RAGE IN CHINESE RESTAURANTS. THE FUROR HAS DIED DOWN, BUT THE DISH NONETHELESS MAKES A SPECTACULAR, FILLING MAIN-COURSE SALAD FOR A WARM-WEATHER LUNCH OR DINNER.

DO NOT USE THE CRISPY FRIED "CHOW MEIN" NOODLES SOLD IN CANS AND SERVED AS A SNACK OR APPETIZER IN OLD-FASHIONED CANTONESE RESTAURANTS. YOU WANT NOODLES YOU HAVE TO COOK BY BOILING. IF YOU CAN'T FIND ANY APPROPRIATE ASIAN NOODLES, USE GOOD OLD ITALIAN PASTA, SUCH AS LINGUINE OR SPAGHETTI.

Italian Steak Salad with Arugula, Gorgonzola, and Balsamic Vinaigrette

SERVES 4

STEAK

1½ pounds flank steak, trimmed of
    visible fat
1 garlic clove, cut in half
2 tablespoons balsamic vinegar
2 tablespoons extra-virgin olive oil
Salt
Black pepper

DRESSING

¼ cup balsamic vinegar
¼ teaspoon salt
¼ teaspoon black pepper
½ teaspoon Dijon mustard
½ cup extra-virgin olive oil

SALAD

4 cups lightly packed arugula leaves
1 red bell pepper, roasted, peeled,
    stemmed, and seeded (see pages
    15–16), torn into thin strips
6 ounces Gorgonzola cheese
¼ cup pine nuts, toasted (see page 17)

1. First, marinate the steak. Rub it lightly all over with the cut sides of the garlic. In a bowl just large enough to hold the meat, stir together the balsamic vinegar and olive oil. Turn the steak in the marinade to coat it well and leave at room temperature for about 30 minutes.

2. Preheat the broiler.

3. Prepare the dressing. In a small mixing bowl, use a fork or small wire whisk to stir together the vinegar, salt, and pepper until the salt dissolves. Add the mustard and stir until thoroughly blended. Stirring continuously, pour in the oil in a thin, steady stream. Set the dressing aside.

4. Season the steak generously all over with salt and black pepper. Broil it until done to your liking, about 2 minutes per side for medium-rare.

5. While the steak cooks, put the arugula leaves and bell pepper strips in a mixing bowl and, tossing continuously,

pour in enough of the dressing to coat them to your liking. Arrange the salad mixture in mounds on large individual serving plates.

6. As soon as the steak is done, carve it crosswise and diagonally into slices no thicker than ¼ inch, immediately draping the slices over the mounds of salad so the meat's juices will mingle with the dressing. Crumble the Gorgonzola over the steak and salad, garnish with pine nuts, and serve immediately.

TEST KITCHEN NOTES

I FIRST ENJOYED A SALAD SIMILAR TO THIS AT A FAVORITE ITALIAN TRATTORIA SEVERAL YEARS AGO, AND I'VE BEEN TINKERING WITH THE CONCEPT EVER SINCE. SEVERAL FACTORS ARE CENTRAL TO MAKING IT MORE THAN JUST A SLAB OF MEAT SERVED ON A PILE OF GREENS. FIRST, MARINATING THE MEAT WITH BALSAMIC VINEGAR AND OLIVE OIL SUBTLY TIES ITS TASTE TO THAT OF THE DRESSING. SECOND, THE CHOICE OF PEPPERY ARUGULA (ALSO KNOWN AS ROCKET), HIGHLIGHTED BY SWEET STRIPS OF ROASTED BELL PEPPER, STANDS UP WELL TO THE MEAT'S ROBUST FLAVOR. FINALLY, GRILLING THE STEAK JUST MOMENTS BEFORE SERVING, AND PLACING THE SLICES ATOP THE GREENS WHILE STILL DRIPPING WITH HOT JUICES, ALLOWS THE FLAVORS TO MINGLE WONDERFULLY.

Oven-fried Chicken on Pickled Vegetable Slaw with Bacon and Pecans

SERVES 4

OVEN-FRIED CHICKEN

¾ cup buttermilk

1 teaspoon salt

¼ teaspoon black pepper

⅛ teaspoon paprika

4 drops hot pepper sauce,
     such as Tabasco

4 large boneless, skinless chicken breast
     halves (about 6 ounces each)

1 cup finely crushed cornflakes

Pinch cayenne pepper

DRESSING

¼ cup cider vinegar

1 teaspoon celery seed

2 teaspoons sugar

½ teaspoon salt

½ teaspoon white pepper

6 tablespoons walnut oil or vegetable oil

SALAD

½ head red cabbage

½ head green cabbage

2 carrots, coarsely shredded

4 whole sweet pickles, coarsely shredded

2 tablespoons finely chopped
     Italian parsley

2 tablespoons finely chopped
     fresh chives

½ pound smoked bacon, thinly sliced

6 cups butter lettuce

¾ cup pecan pieces or halves, toasted
     (see page 17)

Parsley sprigs, for garnish

1. To make the chicken, pour the buttermilk into a mixing bowl and stir in half each of the salt, pepper, and paprika and all of the hot pepper sauce. Trim any traces of fat from the chicken breast halves and add them to the bowl, turning them in the buttermilk to coat completely. Cover the bowl with plastic wrap and refrigerate for at least 1 hour and preferably several hours; turn the chicken breast halves several times during soaking.

2. When you are ready to cook the chicken, preheat the oven to 375°F. Select a baking dish large enough to hold the chicken breasts comfortably in a single layer and spray the inside of the dish with nonstick cooking spray. On a dinner plate or in a shallow bowl placed next to the baking dish, stir together the crushed cornflakes and remaining seasonings, spreading them out in an even bed. One at a time, lift each chicken breast half from the buttermilk and, with your fingertips, turn it in the cornflake mixture to coat it completely and evenly, then place it gently in the baking dish.

When all the chicken breasts have been coated, cover the baking dish with aluminum foil and put it in the preheated oven. Cook the chicken, covered, 20 minutes, then remove the foil and continue cooking until the coating has evenly browned, about 20 minutes more. Remove the chicken and let it cool to room temperature. Refrigerate until serving time.

3. While the chicken is cooking, prepare the dressing and the slaw. For the dressing, in a mixing bowl, use a fork or a small wire whisk to stir together the cider vinegar, celery seed, sugar, salt, and white pepper until the sugar and salt dissolve. Stirring briskly, pour in the oil in a thin, steady stream. Set the dressing aside.

4. Fill a kettle or saucepan with water and bring it to a boil over medium-high heat. Meanwhile, cut the cabbage halves in half again to make quarters and cut out their cores. Place each wedge cut side down on a cutting surface and, with a sharp knife, slice it very thinly to make shreds. Layer the shreds in a large colander or strainer: first the red cabbage, then the green, then the shredded carrot. When the water reaches a boil, hold the colander or strainer over the sink and pour the boiling water slowly, evenly over the vegetables to wilt them. Drain well.

Transfer the wilted vegetables to a large mixing bowl. Add the shredded pickles, the parsley, and the chives. Pour the dressing in and toss thoroughly. Cover the bowl with plastic wrap and refrigerate until serving time.

5. To cook the bacon, arrange the strips side by side in one or two frying pans and cook over medium heat, turning frequently, until crisp and brown, about 10 minutes. Remove the bacon and set aside to drain on several layers of paper toweling.

6. To serve the salad, arrange the butter lettuce leaves to form beds on large, chilled, individual serving plates. Mound the pickled vegetable slaw on each bed of lettuce and crumble the bacon over the slaw. For each serving, slice a chicken breast crosswise into pieces ½-inch thick and arrange them on top of the slaw. Garnish with the pecans and parsley sprigs.

Greek Country-style Lamb Salad

SERVES 4

DRESSING

¼ cup lemon juice

¼ teaspoon salt

¼ teaspoon black pepper

⅛ teaspoon sugar

½ cup extra-virgin olive oil

SALAD

3 ounces uncooked small pasta shells

4 Roma tomatoes, cored and cut into
　　½-inch chunks

1 cucumber, halved lengthwise, seeded,
　　and peeled only if necessary, halves
　　cut crosswise into ½-inch-thick slices

1 green bell pepper, halved, stemmed,
　　seeded, and cut into ½-inch chunks

1 red bell pepper, halved, stemmed,
　　seeded, and cut into ½-inch chunks

½ small red onion, cut into ⅛-inch dice

1 pound cooked lamb, cut into thin,
　　bite-size slices

½ pound feta cheese, crumbled

1 cup Kalamata or other brine-cured
　　black olives, pitted

2 tablespoons fresh oregano leaves,
　　finely chopped, or 1 tablespoon
　　dried oregano, crumbled

4 cups baby salad leaves

4 fresh oregano or parsley sprigs,
　　for garnish

1. To make the dressing, put the lemon juice in a small mixing bowl. Add the salt, pepper, and sugar and, with a fork or small whisk, stir until the salt and sugar dissolve. Stirring continuously, pour in the olive oil until blended. Set the dressing aside.

2. Bring a saucepan of water to a boil. Add the pasta shells and boil until firm-tender but still slightly chewy, 8 to 10 minutes, or according to the suggested time in the package instructions. Drain the pasta in a strainer, rinse well under cold running water, and drain again.

　　Put the pasta in a large mixing bowl and add the tomatoes, cucumber, bell peppers, onion, lamb, feta, olives, and oregano. Add the dressing and toss well to coat the ingredients.

3. Arrange the leaves in beds on large, chilled, individual serving plates or bowls. Distribute the salad mixture equally among the four beds of leaves and garnish with sprigs of parsley.

TEST KITCHEN NOTES

THIS SALAD TAKES ITS INSPIRATION FROM GREECE'S *SALATA HORIATIKI*, LITERALLY "COUNTRY-STYLE SALAD," WHICH IS SERVED IN VIRTUALLY EVERY GREEK *TAVERNA*. A *HORIATIKI* CONSISTS OF SUN-RIPENED TOMATOES, CRISP CUCUMBERS, FETA CHEESE, AND USUALLY SOME CURED OLIVES, DRESSED WITH FRUITY GREEN OLIVE OIL AND LEMON JUICE AND MAYBE SEASONED WITH A LITTLE FRESH OR DRIED OREGANO, GREECE'S UBIQUITOUS HERB.

　　IT TAKES ONLY A VERY SHORT LEAP TO ADD BITE-SIZE SLICES OF LAMB, THE GREEKS' FAVORITE MEAT, WHOSE RICH TASTE GOES PERFECTLY WITH ALL THE OTHER INGREDIENTS. I'VE ALSO INCLUDED A HANDFUL OF SMALL PASTA SHELLS, WHICH CONTRIBUTE ANOTHER SATISFYING TEXTURE AND ADD SOME CARBOHYDRATE TO ROUND OUT THE MEAL. TENDER LETTUCES SUCH AS THE MIXED BABY GREENS CALLED FOR HERE WORK BEST, AS THE SALAD GAINS AMPLE CRISPNESS FROM THE CUCUMBER; YOU COULD ALSO USE BABY SPINACH LEAVES OR A MILDLY BITTER LEAF SUCH AS CHICORY.

　　IDEALLY, YOU WOULD MAKE THIS SALAD THE DAY AFTER YOU HAD SERVED LAMB FOR DINNER, SO DO KEEP THIS RECIPE IN MIND SHOULD YOU EVER ROAST A LEG OF LAMB, WHICH IS BOUND TO LEAVE YOU WITH LEFTOVERS.

Moroccan Grilled Lamb Salad with Couscous and Dried Fruit

SERVES 4

DRESSING

⅓ cup lemon juice

½ tablespoon honey

¼ cup finely chopped fresh mint leaves

⅔ cup extra-virgin olive oil

SALAD

1 pound lamb tenderloin

1 teaspoon vegetable oil

1 teaspoon ground cumin

½ teaspoon ground cinnamon

¼ teaspoon salt

¼ teaspoon black pepper

½ pound dried mixed fruit, such as
    apricots and seedless raisins

2 cups water

2 boxes (about 5½ ounces each)
    quick-cooking couscous

¼ pound pitted dates, coarsely chopped

½ cup slivered almonds, toasted
    (see page 17)

6 cups spinach or other whole,
    medium-size tender salad leaves,
    thoroughly washed

Fresh mint sprigs, for garnish

1. To make the dressing, put the lemon juice in a small mixing bowl, add the honey and stir with a fork or small whisk until the honey dissolves. Stir in the mint. Stirring continuously, slowly pour in the olive oil. Set the dressing aside.

2. To make the salad, first marinate the lamb. In a shallow dish large enough to hold the lamb tenderloin, stir together the oil, cumin, cinnamon, salt, and pepper to form a paste. Rub this paste all over the lamb and leave it to marinate at room temperature for 15 to 30 minutes.

3. Meanwhile, preheat the broiler or grill.

4. While the lamb is marinating, put the dried fruit, excluding the dates, in a bowl or cup and add enough hot tap water to cover them. Leave them to soak until tender, about 10 minutes. Drain well, cut any large pieces into thin strips, and set aside.

5. In a medium-size saucepan, bring the water to a boil over medium-high heat. Stir in the couscous, cover the pan, remove it from the heat, and leave for about 5 minutes, until the couscous is tender. With a table fork, gently fluff the couscous, then transfer it to a large mixing bowl. Add the dried fruit, dates, and almonds and toss gently but thoroughly to combine. Set aside.

6. Grill or broil the lamb until done to your liking, 3 to 4 minutes per side for medium-rare.

7. While the lamb is cooking, arrange the spinach or other salad leaves to form attractive beds on individual large serving plates. Mound the couscous mixture in the center of each plate.

8. Cut the lamb crosswise into ¼- to ½-inch-thick slices and arrange them on top of the couscous. Garnish with mint sprigs and serve immediately.

TEST KITCHEN NOTES

COUSCOUS IS A FORM OF TINY PASTA PELLETS MADE FROM SEMOLINA WHEAT FLOUR. IN ITS TRADITIONAL FORM, THIS NORTH AFRICAN SPECIALTY CAN TAKE QUITE A WHILE TO PREPARE, REQUIRING SLOW STEAMING OVER SIMMERING WATER OR BROTH. THIS RECIPE TAKES ADVANTAGE OF THE QUICK-COOKING VARIETY OF COUSCOUS, WHICH CAN BE MADE IN JUST A FEW MINUTES.

TOSS IN WHATEVER KINDS OF DRIED FRUIT AND NUTS YOU LIKE WITH THE COUSCOUS AND DRESSING. FOR EVEN MORE FLAVOR, YOU COULD USE A LITTLE APPLE JUICE OR SOME WHITE WINE, GENTLY HEATED IN A SMALL SAUCEPAN, TO SOFTEN THE FRUITS.

Grilled Curried Chicken Salad

DRESSING

6 tablespoons plain low-fat or
    nonfat yogurt

6 tablespoons mayonnaise

¼ cup sweet mango chutney, large
    pieces of fruit finely minced

2 tablespoons lemon juice

½ teaspoon salt

½ teaspoon white pepper

SALAD

6 ounces plain low-fat or nonfat yogurt

2 teaspoons curry powder

1 teaspoon finely grated fresh ginger

½ tablespoon lemon juice

4 boneless, skinless chicken breast halves
    (4 to 6 ounces each)

2 large Yukon Gold potatoes or
    other boiling potatoes (about
    6 ounces each)

1 tablespoon vegetable oil

Salt

White pepper

12 cups mixed bitter salad greens such
    as arugula, radicchio, escarole,
    and endive

4 Roma tomatoes, cut into wedges

1 small red onion, thinly sliced

¼ cup light seedless raisins

¼ cup cashew nuts, toasted (see page 17)

¼ cup finely chopped fresh
    cilantro leaves

1. To prepare the dressing, stir together all the ingredients in a small mixing bowl. Cover with plastic wrap and refrigerate.

2. To begin preparing the salad, put the yogurt, curry powder, ginger, and lemon juice in a shallow dish large enough to hold the chicken breast halves in a single layer. Stir well to blend, then add the chicken breast halves and turn to coat them well. Leave to marinate for 15 to 30 minutes.

3. Meanwhile, preheat the broiler or grill.

4. At the same time, cut the potatoes into ½-inch-thick slices and put them in a medium-size saucepan. Add cold water to cover and put the pan over medium-high heat. As soon as the water reaches a boil, drain well.

5. Brush the potato slices with the vegetable oil. Season the chicken breast halves and potatoes with salt and white pepper to taste. Broil or grill the chicken and the potatoes until both are golden brown and the chicken is cooked through, about 5 minutes per side.

6. While the chicken and potatoes are cooking, arrange the salad leaves in beds on large individual serving plates. Cut the chicken breasts crosswise into ½-inch-wide pieces and arrange one on each salad. Place the potato slices and tomato wedges around the chicken. Separate the onion slices into rings and strew them over each salad.

7. Stir the dressing briefly, then drizzle it over each salad. Garnish with raisins, cashews, and cilantro and serve immediately.

TEST KITCHEN NOTES

TANDOORI CHICKEN IS AN INDIAN SPECIALTY IN WHICH CHICKEN PIECES ARE MARINATED IN SPICED YOGURT, THEN COOKED IN A HOT, CHARCOAL-FIRED TANDOOR. USUALLY, INDIAN RESTAURANTS SERVE THE CHICKEN ON A PLATTER GARNISHED WITH LETTUCE, SLICED ONION, AND WEDGES OF TOMATO AND LEMON, WHICH STRIKES ME AS MORE THAN HALFWAY TO BEING A SALAD.

THIS DELIGHTFUL RECIPE TAKES THE CONCEPT THE REST OF THE WAY, WHILE APPROXIMATING TANDOORI CHICKEN'S TENDERNESS, SUCCULENCE, AND SUBTLE SPICE WITHOUT THE USE OF A TANDOOR. THE SAME CURRY TREATMENT ALSO WORKS PERFECTLY WELL WITH LARGE FRESH SHRIMP, OR WITH THIN SLICES OF LAMB TENDERLOIN.

Sautéed Mushroom Salad
with Goat Cheese
and Sun-dried Tomatoes

SERVES 4

12 cups mixed baby salad leaves

12 dry-packed sun-dried tomatoes

6 tablespoons extra-virgin olive oil

4 shallots, finely chopped

1½ pounds mixed mushrooms, tough
    stems removed and discarded,
    caps and tender stems cut into
    ½-inch-thick slices

Salt

Black pepper

¼ cup sherry vinegar or balsamic vinegar

6 tablespoons walnut oil

¼ pound fresh, creamy goat cheese

¼ cup freshly grated Parmesan cheese
    (optional)

½ cup walnuts, toasted (see page 17)

¼ cup finely chopped fresh chives
    or basil

1. Arrange the salad leaves in beds on large individual serving plates.

2. Put the sun-dried tomatoes in a small bowl and add hot tap water to cover. Leave them to soak about 10 minutes, until tender, then drain well and cut the pieces into ¼-inch-wide strips. Set aside.

3. In a large skillet, heat the olive oil over high heat. Add the shallots and, as soon as they sizzle, add the mushrooms. Sauté them, stirring continuously and briskly with a wooden spoon, until they are heated through and their edges begin to brown, 2 to 3 minutes. Stir in the sun-dried tomato pieces and season generously to taste with salt and pepper.

Add the vinegar to the skillet and stir and scrape to deglaze any pan deposits. Stir in the walnut oil.

4. Immediately spoon the mushrooms, sun-dried tomatoes, and hot pan dressing over the beds of salad leaves. Crumble the goat cheese and Parmesan, if desired, over each salad and sprinkle with walnuts and chives or basil. Serve immediately.

Bruschetta Tomato Salad with Prosciutto and Mozzarella

SERVES 4

TOMATO SALAD

16 Roma tomatoes
1 large shallot, finely chopped
½ cup extra-virgin olive oil
¼ cup balsamic vinegar
¼ cup finely chopped Italian parsley
¾ teaspoon salt
½ teaspoon black pepper
½ cup finely shredded fresh basil leaves

TOASTS

32 slices long Italian bread, cut
    diagonally into ½-inch thick slices
¾ cup extra-virgin olive oil
¼ pound prosciutto, very thinly sliced
1 pound fresh mozzarella, thinly sliced

1. To make the tomato salad, first core the tomatoes and cut them in half crosswise. With a fingertip, scoop out and discard the pockets of seeds from each tomato half. Coarsely chop the tomatoes and put them in a mixing bowl. Add the shallot, olive oil, vinegar, parsley, salt, and pepper and toss well. Cover with plastic wrap and marinate in the refrigerator for about 1 hour.

2. Prepare the toasts shortly before serving time. Preheat the grill or broiler. Brush the bread slices on both sides with the olive oil and toast them until golden brown, 2 to 3 minutes per side. If using a grill, distribute the prosciutto and then the cheese evenly over the slices immediately after you turn them over, so the cheese will melt while you toast the undersides. If using a broiler, toast the bread slices on both sides, then remove them from the broiler, top with the prosciutto and cheese, and return them briefly to the broiler until the cheese melts, about 1 minute more.

3. Arrange the toasts, cheese side up, on large individual serving plates. Spoon the tomato salad generously on top of each toast and garnish with the basil. Serve immediately.

TEST KITCHEN NOTES

THE ITALIAN HORS D'OEUVRE OF TOASTED BREAD TOPPED WITH ANY NUMBER OF SAVORY INGREDIENTS HAS BECOME VERY FASHIONABLE IN RECENT YEARS. IN ITS MOST POPULAR FORM, THE BREAD IS SIMPLY RUBBED WITH GARLIC AND OLIVE OIL BEFORE BEING GRILLED OR BROILED, AND IS THEN TOPPED WITH A FRAGRANT MIXTURE OF SUN-RIPENED TOMATOES, GARLIC, HERBS, AND A VINAIGRETTE DRESSING.

THAT SOUNDS SUSPICIOUSLY LIKE A SALAD TO ME. AND, IN FACT, IF YOU TAKE THE SAME BASIC ELEMENTS, CUBE THE BREAD, AND TOSS IT TOGETHER WITH THE TOMATOES, YOU GET AN ITALIAN COUNTRY-STYLE SALAD KNOWN AS *PANZANELLA*. CONSIDERING THAT I'VE OFTEN FOUND A GOOD BRUSCHETTA TO BE THE MOST MEMORABLE PART OF MANY AN ITALIAN MEAL, IT MADE SENSE, THEN, TO TURN IT INTO A MAIN-DISH SALAD THAT, AS A BONUS, YOU COULD CHOOSE TO EAT WITH YOUR HANDS.

Spinach and Goat Cheese Salad with Dried Fruit and Warm Honey-Mustard Vinaigrette

SERVES 4

DRESSING

½ cup balsamic vinegar

2 tablespoons dried cherries

8 dried apricots, cut into ⅛-inch-wide
    slivers

1 teaspoon creamy Dijon mustard

1 teaspoon honey

½ cup extra-virgin olive oil

SALAD

12 cups baby spinach leaves, thoroughly
    washed

1 pound fresh, creamy goat cheese,
    divided into 8 equal rounds

¼ cup extra-virgin olive oil

Salt

White pepper

½ cup pecans, toasted (see page 17)

2 tablespoons finely chopped
    fresh chives

1. To begin making the dressing, put the vinegar in a small saucepan and heat it over medium heat until bubbles begin to appear around its edges. Remove the pan from the heat, add the dried cherries and apricots, cover, and let them steep 10 minutes.

Remove the fruits with a slotted spoon and set them aside. With a small fork or wire whisk, stir the mustard and honey into the pan of vinegar until blended. Stirring continuously over medium-low heat, pour in the oil in a thin, steady stream. Turn off the heat, return the dried fruit to the dressing, and cover the pan.

2. Preheat the broiler.

3. To prepare the salad, arrange the spinach leaves in beds on large individual serving plates.

4. Line a shallow baking dish large enough to hold all the cheese rounds with aluminum foil. Lightly coat each goat cheese round all over with some olive oil and place it on the foil. Sprinkle the cheese rounds lightly with salt and white pepper.

Put the cheese rounds under the broiler, keeping a close eye on them and removing them as soon as they begin to show signs of bubbling and melting, 1 to 2 minutes.

With a spatula, transfer 2 cheese rounds to each bed of spinach. With a large spoon, drizzle the warm dressing and dried fruit evenly over the cheese and spinach. Garnish with pecans and chives. Serve immediately.

TEST KITCHEN NOTES

THIS HEARTY SALAD EXPLODES WITH WONDERFULLY HEADY AROMAS AND FLAVORS: THE TANGY RICHNESS OF THE BUBBLING-HOT GOAT CHEESE, THE INTENSE FRUITINESS OF DRIED CHERRIES AND APRICOTS SOAKED IN BALSAMIC VINEGAR, AND THE SWEET-SPICY TASTE OF THE WARM DRESSING.

BUY A GOOD, FRESH, CREAMY GOAT CHEESE—WHETHER IMPORTED OR DOMESTIC—SHAPED INTO A LOG THAT YOU CAN NEATLY CUT INTO ROUNDS. DEPENDING ON THE BRAND, YOU MIGHT ACTUALLY HAVE TO BUY TWO OR MORE SEPARATE CHEESES TO GET THE REQUIRED AMOUNT.

SUN- OR KILN-DRIED CHERRIES, A SPECIALTY OF THE PACIFIC NORTHWEST, ARE AVAILABLE WITH INCREASING FREQUENCY IN SPECIALTY FOOD STORES AND WELL-STOCKED SUPERMARKETS. IF YOU CAN'T FIND THEM, SUBSTITUTE SEEDLESS RAISINS.

Grilled Pork and Fresh Fig Salad

SERVES 4

DRESSING

¼ cup sherry vinegar

½ teaspoon salt

½ teaspoon sugar

¼ teaspoon black pepper

¼ cup hazelnut or walnut oil

¼ cup vegetable oil

SALAD

¾ pound pork tenderloin, cut into
    ½-inch-thick medallions

1 tablespoon sherry vinegar

1 tablespoon hazelnut or walnut oil

Salt

Black pepper

1 dozen fresh, ripe figs

8 cups baby spinach leaves,
    thoroughly washed

¼ pound fresh, creamy goat cheese

3 ounces hazelnuts, toasted (see page
    17), skinned, and coarsely chopped

1. To make the dressing, put the sherry vinegar in a small mixing bowl. Add the salt, sugar, and pepper and use a fork or small whisk to stir until the salt and sugar dissolve. Stirring continuously, slowly pour in the hazelnut or walnut oil and the vegetable oil. Set the dressing aside until needed.

2. Put the pork medallions in a small bowl and drizzle them with the tablespoon each of sherry vinegar and hazelnut or walnut oil. Turn the medallions to coat them well and leave to marinate at room temperature about 15 minutes.

3. Meanwhile, preheat the grill or broiler. When it is hot, season the pork with salt and pepper and broil until cooked medium to medium-well done, 4 to 5 minutes per side. When you turn the pork over, brush the figs all over with some of the dressing and cook them alongside the pork, turning them frequently to brown evenly.

4. When the pork and figs are done, remove them from the heat. Toss the spinach with enough of the remaining dressing to coat well and arrange it in beds on four large individual serving plates or shallow bowls. With a small, sharp knife, cut each fig lengthwise into quarters. Arrange the pork medallions and figs on top of the spinach. Crumble the goat cheese over each salad and garnish with the hazelnuts. Serve immediately.

TEST KITCHEN NOTES

I FIND PORK TO BE A DELIGHTFULLY ROBUST MEAT WITH AN INHERENT SWEETNESS AND A RICHNESS OF TASTE THAT MAKES IT AN IDEAL CANDIDATE FOR THE STARRING ROLE IN THIS HEARTY MAIN-DISH SALAD.

TO GO WITH THE PORK, I CHOSE SUITABLY FULL-FLAVORED INGREDIENTS: SPINACH, GOAT CHEESE, TOASTED HAZELNUTS, AND, MOST IMPORTANT, FRESH FIGS.

YOU CAN FIND A VARIETY OF FIGS IN WELL-STOCKED PRODUCE DEPARTMENTS AND FARMERS' MARKETS FROM EARLY SUMMER WELL INTO AUTUMN. SELECT ONES THAT ARE FULLY RIPE, PLUMP, AND TENDER TO THE TOUCH, AND THAT HAVE A SWEET AROMA SUGGESTING A COMMENSURATE SWEETNESS OF TASTE. BRIEF GRILLING OF THE FIGS ONLY FURTHER EMPHASIZES THAT NATURAL SWEETNESS BY SLIGHTLY CARAMELIZING THE SUGAR IN THE FRUIT'S OUTERMOST LAYER.

YOU MAY FIND, AS I HAVE, THAT THE FIGS ARE SO SEDUCTIVE AND GO SO WELL WITH THE NUTS AND CHEESE THAT THEY CAN TAKE OVER THE LEAD IN THE SALAD. IF YOU WISH TO LEAVE OUT THE PORK, INCREASE THE QUANTITY OF FIGS BY HALF.

The Baked Potato Salad

SERVES 4

DRESSING

Ranch Dressing (see page 26)

SALAD

4 large baking potatoes

2 tablespoons extra-virgin olive oil

Salt

Black pepper

2 medium-size zucchini, trimmed and
coarsely shredded

2 medium-size carrots, trimmed and
coarsely shredded

1 red bell pepper, quartered, stemmed,
and seeded, quarters cut crosswise
into thin strips

1 small jícama, thickly peeled and
coarsely shredded

¼ pound mushrooms, thinly sliced

¼ cup finely shredded fresh basil or finely
chopped fresh chives

1. Prepare the Ranch Dressing and
set aside.

2. Preheat the oven to 375°F.

3. Rinse the potatoes and lightly
scrub them to remove any dirt. Dry
them well with a kitchen towel or
paper toweling. In a shallow dish, roll
the potatoes all over in the olive oil.
Sprinkle them generously to taste with
salt and pepper.

Place a sheet of foil just big enough
to hold the potatoes on the center rack
of the oven. Put the potatoes on the foil,
not touching each other, and bake until
they feel tender when squeezed with a
pot holder or oven glove and their skins
are nicely browned and crisp.

Remove the potatoes from the oven
and put each in a large, shallow serving
bowl or individual serving plate. With a
small, sharp knife, cut a lengthwise slit
deep into the top of each potato.
Protecting your hands with a folded
kitchen towel, squeeze each potato,
pushing inward from both ends, to open
it wide. With two forks, spread the potato open to make a big, generous pocket.

4. In a mixing bowl, toss together the
prepared raw vegetables. Stuff them into
each potato, allowing the vegetables to
overflow. Drizzle the dressing generously
over each serving and garnish with basil
or chives. Serve immediately.

TEST KITCHEN NOTES

ONE EVENING DURING THE MONTHS WHILE I
WAS DEVELOPING THE RECIPES FOR THIS BOOK,
I POPPED INTO A LOCAL SALAD BAR RESTAU-
RANT AND ACCIDENTALLY CREATED THIS SUR-
PRISINGLY APPEALING SALAD.

I SELECTED A BIG BAKED POTATO, SPLIT IT
OPEN, AND STARTED PILING ON TOP OF IT ALL
SORTS OF SHREDDED AND SLICED RAW VEGETA-
BLES. THEN, I DRIZZLED THE WHOLE THING
WITH RANCH DRESSING, WHICH SEEMED THE
PERFECT COMPLEMENT TO BOTH THE SALAD
AND THE POTATO.

WHAT YOU WILL BE DOING HERE IS USING
THE POTATO AS THE SALAD BOWL.

TAKE THE ACCOMPANYING RECIPE AS A
BASIC FORMULA. SUBSTITUTE ANY OTHER FRESH,
RAW VEGETABLES THAT APPEAL TO YOU, SLICING
OR SHREDDING THEM IN SUCH A WAY THAT
THEY CAN BE STUFFED EASILY INTO THE BAKED
POTATOES AND EATEN WITH A FORK. ADD
SOME SHREDDED OR CRUMBLED CHEESE OF
YOUR CHOICE. IF YOU WANT AN EVEN RICHER
TOPPING, SUBSTITUTE CLASSIC BLUE CHEESE
DRESSING (SEE PAGE 25) FOR THE RANCH.

Grilled Vegetable Salad with Goat Cheese and Pine Nuts

SERVES 4

DRESSING

½ cup balsamic vinegar

½ teaspoon salt

½ teaspoon pepper

¾ cup extra-virgin olive oil

SALAD

2 medium-size zucchini, cut lengthwise
    into ¼-inch-thick slices

2 medium-size crookneck squash, cut
    lengthwise into ¼-inch-thick slices

4 Roma tomatoes, cored and halved
    lengthwise

1 Maui, Vidalia, Walla Walla, or red
    onion, cut crosswise into
    ½-inch-thick slices

1 red bell pepper, quartered, stemmed,
    cored, and seeded, each quarter
    gently flattened

1 dozen large cultivated or cremini
    mushrooms, stems trimmed even
    with caps, or 4 portobello mush-
    rooms, stems removed

12 cups mixed baby salad leaves

3 ounces fresh, creamy goat cheese

¼ cup pine nuts, toasted (see page 17)

¼ cup finely shredded fresh basil leaves

1. First make the dressing. In a small mixing bowl, use a fork or small wire whisk stir together the vinegar, salt, and pepper until the salt dissolves. Stirring continuously, slowly pour in the olive oil.

2. Pour ½ cup of the dressing into a shallow dish large enough to hold all the sliced and whole vegetables comfortably. Add the vegetables and turn to coat them evenly with the dressing. Leave them to marinate while you preheat the grill or broiler.

3. Grill all the vegetables until nicely browned, about 4 minutes per side.

4. While the vegetables are grilling, put the salad leaves in a large mixing bowl and toss them with the remaining dressing until evenly coated. Arrange the leaves in beds on large individual serving plates.

5. As soon as the vegetables are done, arrange them on top of each salad. Crumble the goat cheese over the vegetables. Garnish with pine nuts and basil. Serve immediately.

TEST KITCHEN NOTES

TO ME, THIS SALAD CAPTURES ALL THE GLORY OF FRESH SUMMER PRODUCE: CRISP, TENDER GREENS COATED WITH A SIMPLE, CLEAN-TASTING DRESSING; SUCCULENT VEGETABLES, THEIR FLAVORS INTENSIFIED BY MARINATING THEM IN THE DRESSING AND THEN GRILLING OR BROILING THEM; AND HINTS OF FRESH GOAT CHEESE, PINE NUTS, AND BASIL TO ADD A LITTLE RICHNESS TO THE EXPERIENCE.

IT'S INTERESTING HOW ROBUST THE RESULTS CAN BE. YOU CAN MAKE IT EVEN MORE SO, WHILE STILL RETAINING ITS VEGETARIAN CHARACTER, BY GRILLING A FEW THICK SLICES OF PARBOILED YUKON GOLD POTATO OR OTHER BOILING POTATO. BY ALL MEANS ADD TO THE SALAD ANY OTHER PRODUCE THAT SEEMS APPROPRIATE AND LOOKS GOOD IN THE MARKET, INCLUDING SMALL HEADS OF RADICCHIO OR BELGIAN ENDIVE, HALVED LENGTHWISE; PARBOILED SLICES OF SWEET POTATO OR YAM; COBBETTES OF PARBOILED CORN; WHOLE GREEN ONIONS; AND EVEN LENGTHWISE SLICES OF CARROT OR PARSNIP, WHICH DEVELOP A WONDERFULLY RICH SWEETNESS AS THE INTENSE HEAT CARAMELIZES THEIR NATURAL SUGARS.

CHAPTER 6

Light and Refreshing Salads

Just because a salad is light and refreshing doesn't mean it can't still make a satisfying meal. Witness the main-dish salads on the pages that follow: combinations of fresh fruit with vibrant-tasting dressings or dips; platefuls of delicate vegetables and seafood; cool cucumber salads topped with zestily flavored poultry; salads of cold, wispy pasta garnished with all manner of tempting tidbits.

Each of these salads, and more besides, are bound to bring you satisfaction—not necessarily by filling you up until you can't eat another bite or by chasing away the chill, as do some of the other salads in this book, but by making your taste buds stand to attention and by wafting across your palate like a fresh tropical breeze. Through their imaginative use of seasonings, their sometimes unconventional combinations of ingredients, their often strict attention to seasonality and—sometimes, yes—their sheer audacity, they offer you sensations the likes of which you probably have not enjoyed before. Now that's satisfaction indeed.

Sesame-crusted Salmon Salad

SERVES 4

DRESSING

¼ cup Japanese rice vinegar

½ teaspoon salt

½ teaspoon sugar

¼ teaspoon white pepper

2 tablespoons Asian sesame oil

SALAD

1 pound fresh salmon fillet, cut into 4
    equal pieces

6 tablespoons yellow *miso* paste

2 tablespoons soy sauce

2 teaspoons finely grated fresh ginger

½ cup sesame seeds

12 cups baby spinach leaves, thoroughly
    washed

¼ cup pickled, pink sushi ginger

1. To make the dressing, stir the rice vinegar, salt, sugar, and pepper together in a small mixing bowl until the salt and sugar dissolve. Stirring continuously, slowly pour in the sesame oil. Set the dressing aside.

2. Place each salmon fillet piece flat on a cutting board. With a sharp knife, carefully butterfly each fillet by cutting it horizontally but not completely in half, opening it out to a piece twice its

original dimensions and half its original thickness.

3. In a large, shallow dish or bowl, stir together the *miso*, soy sauce, and ginger. Turn the butterflied salmon fillets in this mixture to coat them evenly.

4. Preheat the broiler. Line a baking dish or baking sheet large enough to hold all the butterflied fillets with aluminum foil. Coat it lightly with nonstick cooking spray.

5. As soon as the broiler is hot, spread the sesame seeds evenly on a plate or other flat surface larger than one butterflied salmon piece. Gently turn each salmon piece in the sesame seeds to coat it evenly, then transfer it to the foil-lined baking dish.

Broil the salmon until it is just cooked through and the sesame crust is golden brown, 3 to 4 minutes per side.

6. While the salmon is broiling, toss the spinach leaves with the reserved dressing and arrange them in beds on large serving plates. Use a spatula to carefully transfer each salmon fillet next to a bed of spinach. Top the salmon with pickled sushi ginger and serve immediately.

TEST KITCHEN NOTES

ALTHOUGH THE CONCEPT OF CRUSTING SALMON FILLETS WITH SESAME SEEDS MIGHT SOUND COMPLICATED, IT IS IN FACT QUITE EASY, MAKING THIS SALAD A CINCH TO PREPARE FOR AN ELEGANT DINNER PARTY AT WHICH YOU WANT TO SERVE YOUR GUESTS SOMETHING SATISFYING AND MEMORABLE.

THE ONLY INGREDIENTS WITH WHICH YOU MIGHT NOT BE FAMILIAR—NAMELY JAPANESE RICE VINEGAR, YELLOW *MISO* (SOYBEAN PASTE), AND PICKLED, PINK SUSHI GINGER—ARE COMMONLY AVAILABLE IN WELL-STOCKED SUPERMARKETS. YOU'LL FIND THE VINEGAR IN THE ASIAN FOODS OR CONDIMENTS AND VINEGARS SECTION, AND THE LATTER TWO IN THE REFRIGERATED CASE. IF YOU CAN'T FIND THE GINGER, SUBSTITUTE LEMON SLICES.

FOR THE SALMON, BUY FILLETS CUT FROM THE CENTER OF THE FISH, WHICH WILL GIVE YOU FAIRLY THICK, UNIFORM PIECES. BEFORE PREPARING THE SALMON, FEEL THE SURFACE OF EACH PIECE WITH YOUR FINGERTIPS IN SEARCH OF ANY ERRANT LITTLE RIB BONES, THEN GRASP THEM BETWEEN YOUR FINGERTIPS, OR WITH A PAIR OF TWEEZERS, AND PULL THEM OUT.

Smoked Salmon and New Potato Salad with Crème Fraîche and Fines Herbes

SERVES 4

2 pounds new potatoes, lightly rinsed
    of any dirt
8 ounces crème fraîche
¼ cup finely minced red onion
1½ tablespoons lemon juice
1 tablespoon finely grated lemon zest
1 tablespoon finely chopped fresh chives
1 tablespoon finely snipped fresh dill
1 tablespoon finely chopped
    Italian parsley
Salt
Black pepper
4 cups mixed baby salad greens
1 pound smoked salmon, thinly sliced
2 lemons, cut into wedges
¼ cup salmon caviar (optional)

1. Put the potatoes in a saucepan of lightly salted water. Bring to a boil over medium-high heat and cook until the potatoes are tender when pierced with the tip of a small, sharp knife, about 10 minutes.

Drain the potatoes well and rinse several times in cold water until they are just cool enough to handle. With a knife, quarter each potato, dropping it into a mixing bowl. Add the crème fraîche, red onion, lemon juice and zest, chives, dill, and parsley. With a spoon, gently mix the ingredients together until the crème fraîche evenly coats the potatoes. Season generously to taste with salt and pepper and gently mix again.

2. Arrange the salad leaves in beds on large, chilled, individual serving plates. Mound the potato salad on each plate. Loosely roll up the smoked salmon slices and drape them over the potatoes on each plate. Nestle lemon wedges nearby for guests to squeeze over their servings. If you like, garnish the salmon with dollops of salmon caviar.

Bay Shrimp and Baby Vegetable Salad

SERVES 4

SALAD

¾ pound assorted baby vegetables

12 cups mixed baby salad leaves

¾ pound cooked bay shrimp

Fresh dill sprigs, for garnish

DRESSING

¼ cup lemon juice

½ teaspoon sugar

½ teaspoon salt

¼ teaspoon white pepper

1 tablespoon finely snipped fresh dill

½ cup extra-virgin olive oil

1. At least 1 hour and up to several hours before serving the salad, use a stovetop steamer to steam the baby vegetables until tender but still crisp; this should take no more than 3 to 5 minutes. Alternatively, put the vegetables in a bowl, add a splash of water, cover with plastic wrap and microwave the vegetables on High until crisp-tender, 1 to 2 minutes, depending on the strength of your oven. When uncovering the vegetables, take care to lift the lid or plastic away from you to avoid being burned by the steam. Transfer the vegetables to a covered bowl and cool in the refrigerator.

2. Before serving the salad, make the dressing. In a small mixing bowl, stir together the lemon juice, sugar, salt, pepper, and dill until the sugar and salt dissolve. Stirring continuously, slowly pour in the olive oil.

Spoon a little of the dressing over the baby vegetables, tossing gently to coat them lightly.

3. Put the salad leaves in a large mixing bowl, add the rest of the dressing, and toss to coat the leaves.

4. Arrange the salad leaves on large, chilled, individual serving plates. If necessary, devein the shrimp. Arrange the baby vegetables and bay shrimp on top. Garnish with dill sprigs and serve immediately.

TEST KITCHEN NOTES

COOKS HAVE FALLEN IN LOVE WITH ALL THE BABY VEGETABLES AND BABY SALAD GREENS LATELY, SO THIS RECIPE WAS CREATED TO CELEBRATE THESE SUCCULENT MORSELS.

BABY SUMMER SQUASHES, INCLUDING ZUCCHINI, CROOKNECKS, AND ACORNS; BABY CARROTS AND DOLLHOUSE-SIZE CAULIFLOWER; BABY BEETS BARELY BIGGER THAN A MARBLE: ALL, AND MORE, ARE FAIR GAME. SO, TOO, ARE ANY TINY BITES OF VEGETABLE YOU MIGHT CARE TO CONSTRUCT FROM LARGER ONES YOU BUY, SUCH AS SMALL FLORETS OF BROCCOLI, THE LITTLEST SNOW PEAS YOU CAN SELECT FROM THE STALL, OR THE SMALL, PERFECTLY WHITTLED-DOWN LITTLE JUVENILE CARROTS YOU SOMETIMES FIND PACKAGED IN THE PRODUCE SECTION.

BABY BAY SHRIMP, BOUGHT PRECOOKED FROM THE SEAFOOD DEPARTMENT, ARE THE PERFECT TOPPING. ADD A LEMON-DILL VINAIGRETTE AND YOU HAVE THE LIGHTEST MAIN-DISH SALAD IMAGINABLE.

Seared Ahi Tuna Salad with Wasabi Dressing

SERVES 4

DRESSING

1 tablespoon *wasabi* powder
½ tablespoon cold water
1 tablespoon *tamari*
1 tablespoon lemon juice

SALAD

2 tablespoons seasoned rice vinegar
2 tablespoons *tamari*
2 tablespoons toasted sesame oil
¾ pound fresh ahi tuna fillet
4 small heads butter lettuce,
    leaves separated
¼ cup pickled, pink sushi ginger
¼ cup finely chopped fresh chives
¼ cup sesame seeds, toasted
    (see page 17)

1. First, make the dressing. In a small bowl, stir together the *wasabi* powder and water until they form a smooth paste. Stir in the *tamari* and lemon juice, cover, and refrigerate.

2. To prepare the ahi, put the rice vinegar, *tamari*, and sesame oil in a shallow bowl large enough to hold the fillet, and stir them together. Add the ahi and turn to coat it with the marinade. Cover the bowl and refrigerate for 1 hour.

3. Before serving, sort through the butter lettuce leaves, selecting the best specimens, and arrange them in beds on large, chilled, individual serving plates.

4. Over medium-high heat, heat a small nonstick skillet just large enough to hold the ahi fillet. Put the fillet in the pan and sear it for 30 to 45 seconds per side.

Remove the fillet from the pan. If it is wide, cut it in half lengthwise. Cut it crosswise into ¼-inch-thick slices.

5. Arrange the ahi slices on top of the butter lettuce leaves. Drizzle the dressing evenly over the ahi and garnish each piece with some pickled ginger, chives, and sesame seeds. Serve immediately.

TEST KITCHEN NOTES

IF YOU'RE A LOVER OF SUSHI, THIS IS ABSOLUTELY THE MAIN-DISH SALAD FOR YOU. FINE, RAW AHI TUNA IS MARINATED HERE IN A MIXTURE OF SEASONED RICE VINEGAR, SOY SAUCE, AND TOASTED SESAME OIL—ALL READILY AVAILABLE IN THE ASIAN FOOD SECTION OF WELL-STOCKED SUPERMARKETS—AND THEN BRIEFLY SEARED ON ALL SIDES OVER HIGH HEAT TO SEAL IN THE FLAVORINGS WITHOUT REALLY COOKING THE FISH. THEN, THE TUNA IS CUT INTO BITE-SIZE SLICES AND ARRANGED ATOP SMALL LEAVES OF BUTTER LETTUCE, HIGHLIGHTING THE FISH'S BEAUTIFUL DEEP RED COLOR. FINALLY, THE TUNA IS GARNISHED WITH PICKLED GINGER, CHIVES, SESAME SEEDS, AND A DRESSING FLAVORED WITH *WASABI*—A FIERY GREEN JAPANESE HORSERADISH POWDER FOUND, LIKE THE GINGER, IN WELL-STOCKED SUPERMARKETS.

BE SURE TO BUY YOUR AHI FROM THE ABSOLUTELY FINEST, MOST RELIABLE FISHMONGER. THE FILLET SHOULD BE UNDENIABLY FRESH, FREE OF ANY "OFF" AROMA. YOU MIGHT EVEN CONSIDER TRYING TO BUY THE AHI FROM A SUSHI BAR YOU KNOW AND TRUST. *IF YOU HAVE ANY DOUBTS ABOUT THE FRESHNESS OR PURITY OF THE FISH, AVOID IT.*

Shrimp-and-Pasta-Shell Pineapple Boats

SERVES 4

SALAD

2 medium-size whole ripe pineapples
    with leaves attached

6 ounces dried small pasta shells

¾ pound cooked bay shrimp

1 can (8 ounces) sliced water chestnuts,
    drained

1 red bell pepper, quartered, stemmed,
    seeded, and cut into ¼-inch dice

½ small red onion, finely chopped

1 teaspoon salt

1 teaspoon white pepper

Fresh mint sprigs, for garnish

DRESSING

¾ cup mayonnaise

2 tablespoons frozen orange juice
    concentrate, defrosted

2 tablespoons lemon juice

2 tablespoons grated lemon zest

1 tablespoon finely chopped fresh
    cilantro leaves

1 tablespoon finely chopped fresh
    mint leaves

1. Using a large, sharp knife, carefully cut the pineapples in half, cutting from their stalk ends evenly through the fruit and through their crowns of leaves (see Test Kitchen Notes). Using a small, sharp knife and carefully working in small sections at a time, cut out the fruit from each half, leaving a shell about ½-inch thick. Cut out and discard the tough central core from the fruit you remove. Coarsely chop the fruit and transfer it to a large mixing bowl. Holding each pineapple half over the bowl, use your fingertips or a spoon to scrape the juice from some of the fruit that remains clinging to the shell, letting the juice drop into the bowl. Cover the bowl of fruit and the hollowed-out pineapple boats with plastic wrap and refrigerate.

2. Bring a large saucepan of water to a boil. Add the pasta shells and cook until firm-tender but still chewy, 8 to 10 minutes, or according to the package directions. Drain the shells, rinse under cold running water to cool them, then drain well again.

3. Transfer the pasta shells to the bowl of chopped pineapple. Add the shrimp, water chestnuts, bell pepper, and onion. Sprinkle on the salt and white pepper and toss to mix.

4. Prepare the dressing. In a small mixing bowl, stir together the mayonnaise, orange juice concentrate, lemon juice and zest, cilantro, and mint. Pour this dressing over the pineapple mixture and toss well to coat the ingredients.

5. To serve the salads, place a pineapple boat on each large individual serving plate or bowl. With a large spoon, fill each boat with the salad, mounding the mixture generously above the rim of the boat. Garnish with mint sprigs and serve immediately.

TEST KITCHEN NOTES

THE CROWN OF SPIKY LEAVES LOOKS ESPECIALLY PRETTY WHEN YOU'VE CUT THE PINEAPPLES LENGTHWISE IN HALF TO MAKE THE BOATS, SO DON'T CUT THE TOP OFF. CUTTING THE PINEAPPLE IS AN AWKWARD JOB. USE A LARGE, SHARP, SERRATED BREAD KNIFE AND WORK ON A NONSLIP CUTTING BOARD. BE SURE ALWAYS TO CUT AWAY FROM YOURSELF AND TO KEEP YOUR FINGERS WELL CLEAR OF THE KNIFE WHILE YOU STEADY THE FRUIT. TAKE EQUAL CARE WHEN HOLLOWING OUT EACH PINEAPPLE HALF, CUTTING OUT THE FRUIT IN SECTIONS TO MAINTAIN THE INTEGRITY OF THE BOATS AND THE SAFETY OF YOUR HANDS.

Bravocado

SALAD

4 cups mixed salad greens

2 large, ripe Haas avocados

1 lemon, cut in half

2 navel oranges

¾ pound cooked lump crabmeat,
   sorted to remove all bits of shell
   and cartilage

¾ pound cooked bay shrimp

1 small red onion, cut into very thin slices

2 tablespoons finely chopped
   Italian parsley

2 tablespoons finely chopped
   fresh chives

DRESSING

Juice reserved from segmenting oranges

½ cup mayonnaise

¾ cup bottled cocktail sauce

1. To assemble the salad, arrange the greens to form beds in large, chilled, shallow individual serving bowls.

2. Cut each avocado in half and remove the pit. Rub the exposed surfaces of the avocado halves generously with the cut lemon, gently squeezing the lemon halves as you do. Nestle an avocado half in each bed of lettuce.

3. With a sharp knife, cut off the stem and navel ends of the oranges in slices thick enough to reveal the fruit; reserve the slices. One at a time, stand the oranges on their navel ends and cut off the peel in strips thick enough to remove the membranes and reveal the fruit; reserve the peel. Holding each orange in your hand over a small mixing bowl, use a small, sharp knife to cut between the fruit and membrane of each segment, allowing it to drop into the bowl.

Remove the orange segments from the bowl and arrange them around the avocado halves. Take the reserved strips of peel and squeeze them gently over the bowl, one at a time, to extract the juice from the fruit that adheres to them. Set the bowl of juice aside.

4. In another bowl, toss together the crabmeat and shrimp. Pile the seafood into the center of each avocado half, allowing it to tumble over onto the bed of greens. Strew the sliced red onion on top.

5. Into the bowl of orange juice stir the mayonnaise and cocktail sauce to make a creamy but fluid dressing. Drizzle the dressing all over each salad. Garnish with parsley and chives and serve immediately.

TEST KITCHEN NOTES

THIS DELICIOUS SALAD WILL ELICIT BRAVOS FROM EVEN THE MOST DISCRIMINATING OF DINNER GUESTS.

THIS RECIPE BEGINS WITH THE TYPICAL SEAFOOD-STUFFED AVOCADO, BUT THEN TAKES THE CONCEPT SEVERAL STEPS FURTHER BY ADDING THE SPARK OF RED ONION AND SWEET ORANGE SEGMENTS, THEN DRESSING THE ENTIRE SALAD WITH AN APPEALINGLY SWEET-TANGY BLEND OF SEAFOOD COCKTAIL SAUCE, MAYONNAISE, AND ORANGE JUICE.

THE SALAD GOES TOGETHER VERY QUICKLY, SINCE YOU'RE USING READY-PREPARED INGREDIENTS: COOKED LUMP CRABMEAT AND BAY SHRIMP, AND COMMERCIAL MAYONNAISE AND SEAFOOD COCKTAIL SAUCE. THE MOST ARDUOUS WORK YOU HAVE TO DO IS CUT OUT THE ORANGE SEGMENTS, WHICH TAKES BUT A FEW MINUTES AND YIELDS THE JUICE THAT THINS AND SWEETENS THE DRESSING.

YOU COULD MAKE THE SALAD, IF YOU LIKE, ENTIRELY WITH CRAB OR SHRIMP. AS YOU WOULD WHENEVER USING AVOCADO IN A SALAD, ALWAYS START WITH THE DARK, BUMPY-SKINNED HAAS VARIETY, WHICH WILL GIVE YOU THE BEST FLAVOR AND TEXTURE.

Broiled Crab Cake Salad with Napa Cabbage and Lemon-Mustard-Cream Dressing

SERVES 4

DRESSING

¼ cup lemon juice

¾ teaspoon sugar

¼ teaspoon salt

¼ teaspoon white pepper

2 teaspoons grainy Dijon mustard

1 cup heavy cream

1 tablespoon finely chopped fresh basil

1 tablespoon finely chopped fresh chives

SALAD

¾ pound freshly cooked lump crabmeat,
   sorted to remove pieces of shell and
   cartilage

2 large eggs, lightly beaten

1 cup fine, fresh, white bread crumbs

½ cup mayonnaise

6 tablespoons whipping cream

3 tablespoons finely chopped fresh chives

3 tablespoons finely chopped fresh
   Italian parsley

1 large ripe Haas avocado

1 tablespoon lemon jusice

2 heads napa cabbage

2 roasted red peppers, cut into strips
   (see pages 15–16)

12 sprigs fresh watercress, for garnish

1 lemon, cut into 8 wedges, for garnish

1. First, make the dressing. In a mixing bowl, use a wire whisk to stir together the lemon juice, sugar, salt, and pepper until the sugar and salt dissolve. Add the mustard and stir until blended. Whisking continuously, slowly pour in the cream, continuing to whisk until the mixture is thick but still fluid. Stir in the herbs. Cover the bowl and refrigerate.

2. To make the crab cake mixture, put the crabmeat, eggs, bread crumbs, mayonnaise, cream, chives, and parsley in a mixing bowl. With your hands, mix them together until well blended. Cover with plastic wrap and refrigerate until chilled, at least 1 hour.

3. Preheat the broiler. Line a baking sheet large enough to hold all the crab cakes with aluminum foil. Spray the foil with nonstick cooking spray.

4. Halve the avocado and remove the pit. Cut each half lengthwise into 6 thin wedges and remove the peel from each.

Put the lemon juice in a shallow bowl and gently turn the avocado wedges in it to coat them.

5. Using a ¼-cup measure, form 12 crab cakes about 2 inches in diameter and 1 inch thick, placing them on the foil-lined sheet.

6. Cut the heads of cabbage crosswise into strips about ½-inch wide. Discard the cores. Put the cabbage strips in a mixing bowl, add the dressing, and toss well to coat the cabbage. Arrange the cabbage in beds on large, chilled, individual serving plates.

7. Broil the crab cakes until golden brown, about 3 minutes per side. Place 3 crab cakes on each bed of cabbage. Garnish each plate with avocado slices, roasted pepper strips, and watercress sprigs. Place 2 wedges of lemon on each plate for each person to squeeze over the crab cakes to taste. Serve immediately.

TEST KITCHEN NOTES

BUY THE BEST COOKED LUMP CRABMEAT YOU CAN FIND. MEAT TAKEN FROM CRAB LEGS, SOLD COOKED AT MANY SEAFOOD COUNTERS, ALSO WORKS WELL; JUST MAKE SURE TO ASK THAT THE LEGS BE CRACKED FOR YOU AT THE STORE, SO YOU CAN EXTRACT THE MEAT MORE EASILY AT HOME.

Seafood Louis

DRESSING

½ cup mayonnaise

¾ cup bottled cocktail sauce

2 tablespoons lemon juice

SALAD

12 cups romaine, torn into bite-size
    pieces

1 large, ripe Haas avocado

1 tablespoon lemon juice

¾ pound lump crabmeat, sorted to
    remove all bits of shell and cartilage

¾ pound cooked bay shrimp

3 Roma tomatoes, cored and cut into
    quarters

3 large eggs, hard-cooked, shelled, and
    cut into quarters

Italian parsley sprigs, for garnish

1. First, make the dressing. Put the mayonnaise, cocktail sauce, and lemon juice in a small mixing bowl and stir well until blended. Set aside.

2. Arrange the lettuce in beds on large, chilled, individual serving plates or bowls.

3. Halve the avocado and remove the pit. Cut each half lengthwise into 6 thin wedges and remove the peel from each. Put the lemon juice in a shallow bowl and gently turn the avocado wedges in it to coat them.

4. Arrange the crabmeat and shrimp on top of each bed of lettuce. Place 3 avocado wedges, 3 tomato wedges, and 3 wedges of egg on each plate. Drizzle the dressing over each serving, garnish with parsley, and serve immediately.

TEST KITCHEN NOTES

THIS IS THE SORT OF MAIN-DISH SALAD YOU ARE LIKELY TO ENCOUNTER ON THE LUNCHEON MENU OF A GOOD OLD-FASHIONED ROADHOUSE GRILL. NOTHING IN THE RECIPE IS OUT OF THE ORDINARY; EVERY INGREDIENT IS REASSURINGLY FAMILIAR.

IN PLACE OF THE LUMP CRABMEAT, I HAVE HAD GREAT SUCCESS MAKING THIS SALAD WITH MEAT EXTRACTED FROM COOKED CRAB LEGS THAT I BOUGHT AT THE SEAFOOD COUNTER OF A LOCAL SUPERMARKET. BE SURE TO ASK THE COUNTER PERSON TO CRACK THE LEGS WITH A MALLET BEFORE THEY ARE WRAPPED UP FOR YOU, WHICH MAKES IT MUCH EASIER TO EXTRACT THE MEAT BY HAND. OF COURSE, YOU COULD MAKE THIS SALAD ENTIRELY WITH CRAB ALONE OR WITH SHRIMP; AND IF FRESHLY COOKED LOBSTER MEAT OR OTHER SHELLFISH LIKE SCALLOPS, CRAYFISH, OR LANGOUSTINE ARE AVAILABLE, DON'T HESITATE TO SUBSTITUTE THEM.

AS A CLASSIC ROADHOUSE GRILL MIGHT, SERVE THIS SALAD WITH HOT, CRUSTY SOURDOUGH BREAD.

Vietnamese Rock Shrimp and Rice Stick Salad

SERVES 4

DRESSING

¾ cup seasoned rice vinegar

6 tablespoons finely minced pickled, pink sushi ginger

3 fresh serrano chilies

1 tablespoon toasted sesame oil

SALAD

2 packages (6 ounces each) rice sticks

2 medium-size heads napa cabbage

2 carrots

1 Japanese or hothouse (English) cucumber

¾ pound cooked shelled rock shrimp

¼ cup finely chopped fresh mint leaves

¼ cup finely shredded fresh basil leaves

½ cup dry-roasted peanuts

1. First, make the dressing. Put the rice vinegar in a small mixing bowl and stir in the ginger. Stem and halve the chilies (make sure to wash your hands thoroughly after handling chilies, avoiding contact with the sensitive skin around your eys, nose, and mouth before you do). If you want a hotter dressing, leave the seeds in; if not, remove them. Finely mince the chilies and add them to the bowl. Stir in the sesame oil and set the dressing aside.

2. To make the salad, first prepare the rice sticks. Bring a kettle of water to a boil. Meanwhile, put the rice sticks in a large strainer and rinse well with cold running water. Transfer them to a large bowl. Pour boiling water over them until they are submerged. Leave them to soak for 1 minute, then drain immediately in the strainer and rinse with cold running water to cool them. Drain again.

3. With a large knife, cut the napa cabbage heads crosswise into thin shreds, discarding the cores. Arrange the shreds to form beds on large individual serving plates.

4. Using the fine holes on a grater, grate the carrots lengthwise into thin shreds. Arrange the carrot shreds on top of the cabbage shreds, leaving a ring of cabbage showing.

5. Arrange the rice sticks in a bed on top of the carrots, leaving a ring of carrots showing.

6. Using the larger holes of the grater, grate the cucumber lengthwise into thicker shreds. Arrange the cucumber

shreds to form nests on top of the rice sticks, leaving a ring of rice sticks showing.

7. Place the rock shrimp atop the nest of cucumber shreds.

8. Spoon the dressing evenly all over the salads. Garnish with the mint and basil and scatter the peanuts on top. Serve immediately.

> ### TEST KITCHEN NOTES
>
> YOU CAN FIND THE INGREDIENTS FOR THIS SALAD WITHOUT TOO MUCH TROUBLE. MOST SUPERMARKETS CARRY RICE STICKS, SEASONED RICE VINEGAR, AND TOASTED SESAME OIL IN THEIR ASIAN FOODS SECTIONS; IF NOT, SEEK OUT ANY ASIAN MARKET AND YOU'LL FIND THEM THERE. PICKLED PINK SUSHI GINGER SLICES CAN BE FOUND IN THE REFRIGERATED CASE AT THE SUPERMARKET OR AT AN ASIAN MARKET. IF YOU CAN'T FIND A SMALL, HOT SERRANO CHILI, USE HALF TO A THIRD OF A FRESH JALAPEÑO. AS FOR THOSE RICE STICKS, YOU MAY ALSO FIND THEM UNDER THE CHINESE NAME *MAI FUN*. THEY LOOK LIKE THINLY SPUN THREADS, AS FINE AS ANGEL HAIR PASTA. MADE FROM ALREADY COOKED RICE, THEY REQUIRE JUST A BRIEF SOFTENING WITH BOILING WATER.

Grilled Scallop and Maui Onion Ring Salad

SERVES 4

6. Separate the grilled onion slices into rings and strew them over the salads (a fork may help you do this, as they will be hot). With a sharp knife, cut each scallop horizontally into two thinner disks. Arrange the disks of scallop golden sides up on top of the salads. Scatter the pine nuts on top and strew with fresh basil shreds. Serve immediately.

DRESSING

¼ cup balsamic vinegar
½ teaspoon salt
¼ teaspoon black pepper
¾ cup extra-virgin olive oil

SALAD

2 tablespoons lemon juice
4 tablespoons extra-virgin olive oil
¾ pound sea scallops, trimmed of any
    tough white connective tissue
1 large Maui onion
Salt
White pepper
12 cups mixed baby salad leaves
6 ounces baby yellow teardrop or golden
    plum or cherry tomatoes
¼ cup pine nuts, toasted (see page 17)
3 tablespoons finely shredded fresh
    basil leaves

1. First, make the dressing. In a small mixing bowl, stir together with a fork or small wire whisk the balsamic vinegar, salt, and black pepper until the salt dissolves. Stirring continuously, add the olive oil in a thin, steady stream. Set aside.

2. To prepare the salad, stir together in a small bowl the lemon juice and half the olive oil. Then add the scallops, turning to coat them. Leave them to marinate at room temperature while you preheat the grill or broiler.

3. Slice off the stem and root ends of the Maui onion. Cut the onion crosswise into slices ¼ to ½ inch thick. Brush the slices on both sides with the remaining olive oil.

4. Sprinkle the scallops and onion slices to taste with salt and white pepper and grill or broil them until they are lightly golden brown, 2 to 3 minutes per side.

5. Meanwhile, put the salad leaves and tomatoes in a large mixing bowl and toss with enough dressing to coat them well. Arrange the leaves and tomatoes in attractive beds on large individual serving plates.

TEST KITCHEN NOTES

I OWE THE INSPIRATION FOR THIS SALAD TO MY FRIEND AND COLLEAGUE MICHAEL MCCARTY, OWNER OF THE ACCLAIMED MICHAEL'S RESTAURANTS IN SANTA MONICA AND NEW YORK CITY.

THIS VERSION FEATURES THE EYE-OPENING FLAVOR COMBINATIONS OF MICHAEL'S SEAFOOD SALADS, BUT SIMPLIFIES THE PROCEDURE AND CHANGES SOME OF THE MORE ELABORATE RESTAURANT INGREDIENTS AND PRESENTATION STYLE. YOU COULD SUBSTITUTE CHERRY TOMATOES OR EVEN SLICED ROMA TOMATOES FOR THE LITTLE YELLOW TEARDROPS I CALL FOR. OTHER SWEET ONIONS SUCH AS WALLA WALLA, VIDALIA, OR PLAIN OLD RED ONION COULD STAND IN FOR THE MAUI. FOR THAT MATTER, YOU COULD USE MEDIUM-TO-LARGE FRESH SHRIMP INSTEAD OF THE SCALLOPS, ALTHOUGH THE MILKY SWEETNESS AND TENDER TEXTURE OF THE LATTER GO SO VERY WELL WITH THE GRILLED ONIONS AND SHARP-TASTING PINE NUTS.

Grilled Chicken and Orange Salad on Baby Spinach

SERVES 4

4 navel oranges, or other sweet, juicy
    oranges
¾ teaspoon salt
¾ teaspoon black pepper
1 cup extra-virgin olive oil
4 boneless, skinless chicken breast halves
    (4 to 6 ounces each)
6 cups baby spinach leaves, thoroughly
    washed
½ small red onion, very thinly sliced

1. With a sharp knife, cut a slice off the stem and flower ends of each orange thick enough to expose the fruit beneath its outer membrane; set the slices aside. Stand each orange on a sliced end and, cutting from top to bottom, slice off the remainder of the peel in strips thick enough to remove all the white pith and outer membrane, revealing the fruit; reserve the strips of peel. Cut each orange crosswise into slices about ½ inch thick; set the larger slices aside, reserving the smaller top and bottom slices of fruit along with the pieces of peel.

2. Over a mixing bowl, use your hands to tightly squeeze the top and bottom slices of fruit to extract their juice. Likewise, squeeze the pieces of orange peel to extract juice from any fruit pulp adhering to their insides. Discard the peels.

3. Add the salt and pepper to the orange juice and stir with a fork or wire whisk until the salt dissolves. Stirring continuously, slowly pour in the olive oil.

4. Pour half of the resulting dressing into another mixing bowl. Add the chicken breasts and turn to coat them well. Leave to marinate for about 15 minutes.

5. Meanwhile, preheat the broiler or grill.

6. Remove the chicken breasts from the marinade and discard the marinade. Season the chicken breasts with salt and pepper to taste. Broil or grill the chicken breasts until done, about 5 minutes per side. When you turn the chicken over to cook on the second side, dip the orange slices in the reserved dressing and cook them alongside the chicken until golden, 2 to 3 minutes per side.

7. Toss the spinach leaves with the dressing and arrange them in beds on large, chilled, individual serving plates. Cut each chicken breast crosswise into ½-inch-wide slices and arrange them and the orange slices on top of the spinach. Strew each salad with red onions and serve immediately.

TEST KITCHEN NOTES

AS LIGHT ON THE PALATE AS IT IS ON THE STOMACH, THIS SALAD IS THE IDEAL MAIN COURSE FOR A SPECIAL-OCCASION, WARM-WEATHER LUNCHEON. THE FLAVORS ARE SPRIGHTLY, YET COMPLEX AND SATISFYING. THE ARRAY OF BRIGHT COLORS AND PLEASING SHAPES JUST COULDN'T BE PRETTIER. DEPENDING UPON YOUR PREFERENCE AND THE STYLE OF THE OCCASION, YOU CAN PRESENT THE SALADS WITH THEIR INGREDIENTS NEATLY ARRANGED ATOP THE SPINACH, AS THE INSTRUCTIONS HERE CALL FOR, OR ALL TOSSED TOGETHER.

Lemon Chicken Pasta Salad

SERVES 4

DRESSING

¼ cup lemon juice

½ teaspoon sugar

½ teaspoon salt

¼ teaspoon white pepper

1 tablespoon Dijon mustard

1 tablespoon finely chopped Italian
    parsley

1 tablespoon finely snipped fresh dill

1 tablespoon finely shredded fresh basil
    leaves

¾ cup extra-virgin olive oil

SALAD

1 pound boneless, skinless chicken
    breast halves

2 tablespoons lemon juice

1 tablespoon grated lemon zest

1 teaspoon sugar

2 tablespoons olive oil

¾ pound dried rainbow fusilli

2 dozen large pitted black olives, broken
    in half

2 whole roasted red bell peppers, cut
    into thin strips

½ small red onion, cut into very thin slices

6 cups mixed salad leaves

¼ cup pine nuts, toasted (see page 17)

1. Prepare the dressing. In a small bowl, stir together with a fork or small wire whisk the lemon juice, sugar, salt, and pepper until the sugar and salt dissolve. Stir in the mustard until blended, then stir in the parsley, dill, and basil. Stirring continuously, slowly pour in the olive oil. Set the dressing aside.

2. To make the salad, first marinate the chicken breasts. In a shallow dish large enough to hold the chicken in a single layer, stir together the lemon juice and zest and the sugar until the sugar dissolves; then stir in the olive oil. Add the chicken breast halves and turn to coat them. Leave them to marinate for 15 to 30 minutes.

3. Meanwhile, preheat the broiler or grill.

4. At the same time, bring a large pot of water to a boil over medium-high heat. Add the pasta and cook until firm-tender but still chewy, 7 to 9 minutes or according to the package instructions.

Drain the pasta in a strainer, rinse under cold running water until it is cool, then drain well again. Transfer the pasta to a large mixing bowl, add 2 tablespoons of the dressing, and toss well.

5. When the chicken is done, cut each breast half lengthwise in half again; then cut these strips crosswise into ½-inch-wide pieces. Add them to the bowl of pasta and also add the black olives, roasted pepper strips, onion, and remaining dressing. Toss well to coat all the ingredients. If not serving the salad immediately, cover the bowl with plastic wrap and refrigerate.

6. To serve, arrange the salad leaves in beds on large, chilled, individual serving plates or shallow bowls. Mound the pasta salad on top and garnish with pine nuts.

TEST KITCHEN NOTES

I THINK OF THIS AS THE QUINTESSENTIAL MAIN-COURSE PASTA SALAD FOR MANY REASONS. IT IS FILLING, AS ALL GOOD PASTA SALADS SHOULD BY NATURE BE, YET IT IS LIGHT AND REFRESHING IN ITS FLAVORS, A PERFECT DISH TO SERVE WHEN THE WEATHER IS WARM OR WHEN YOU WISH IT WAS.

Japanese Chicken Salad

SERVES 4

CHICKEN

1¾ cups chicken broth

1 tablespoon soy sauce

4 thin slices fresh ginger

¾ pound chicken tenders

SALAD

¼ cup Japanese rice vinegar

1 teaspoon sugar

1 teaspoon salt

2 medium-size Japanese cucumbers, cut
   crosswise into very thin slices

¾ pound Japanese *soba* noodles

1 tablespoon toasted sesame oil

1 teaspoon soy sauce

1 small carrot, finely shredded

1 green onion, thinly sliced

2 teaspoons sesame seeds, toasted
   (see page 17)

1. Prepare the chicken at least 2 hours and up to 24 hours before serving time. Put the chicken broth, soy sauce, and ginger slices in a medium-size saucepan and bring to a boil over medium-high heat. Reduce the heat to very low, add the chicken tenders, cover, and poach until cooked through, about 10 minutes. Let the chicken cool in the broth at room temperature for about 30 minutes, then transfer the chicken and broth to a bowl, cover with plastic wrap, and refrigerate until cold.

2. At least 30 minutes before serving time, prepare the cucumbers. Put the rice vinegar in a mixing bowl and stir in the sugar and salt until dissolved. Add the cucumber slices and toss well. Cover with plastic wrap and refrigerate until serving time.

3. To assemble the salad, bring a large saucepan of water to a boil over medium-high heat. Add the *soba* and boil until tender but still slightly chewy, about 5 minutes or according to the package directions. Drain well in a strainer, then rinse under cold running water until cool and drain well again. Transfer the noodles to a bowl and stir in the sesame oil and soy sauce.

4. Arrange the noodles in beds on four large individual serving plates. Distribute the cucumber salad on top of the noodles. Remove the chicken tenders from the broth, reserving the broth for another use, if you wish. Cut the tenders crosswise into ½-inch pieces and arrange them on top of the cucumbers. Garnish with shredded carrot, green onion, and sesame seeds and serve immediately.

TEST KITCHEN NOTES

As exotic as this salad may seem, all its ingredients can be found in the Asian foods section of a well-stocked supermarket.

The bed of dark brown buckwheat noodles lends a pleasingly earthy base to a refreshing and light-tasting mixture of crisp cucumbers, poached chicken, and hints of rice vinegar, soy sauce, and sesame.

For the chicken, I like to use breast tenders, the long, thin strips of white meat detached from the breast and, in many meat departments, sold separately at a reasonable price. If using whole, boneless, skinless breasts instead, increase the poaching time by about 5 minutes and, after cooking, cut the breasts in half lengthwise before cutting crosswise into chunks.

This salad presentation also works very well with fresh, medium-size shrimp. Peel and devein them, leaving the tail fins intact, and poach them for about half the time required to cook the chicken tenders.

Grilled Duck Sausage Salad with Fresh Pear and Berry Vinaigrette

SERVES 4

DRESSING

6 tablespoons raspberry vinegar
½ teaspoon salt
¼ teaspoon white pepper
½ cup extra-virgin olive oil

SALAD

4 fresh duck sausages
    (about 4 ounces each)
1 medium-size red onion, cut into
    ¼- to ½-inch-thick slices
2 tablespoons extra-virgin olive oil
Salt
White pepper
6 cups arugula leaves
6 cups radicchio leaves, torn into
    bite-size pieces
2 large firm but ripe pears
6 ounces fresh, or frozen and thawed,
    raspberries
¼ cup pine nuts, toasted (see page 17)
¼ cup finely shredded fresh basil leaves

1. Prepare the dressing. In a small bowl, stir together the raspberry vinegar, salt, and white pepper until the salt dissolves. Stirring continuously, pour in the oil in a thin, steady stream. Set the dressing aside.

2. Preheat the grill or broiler.

3. Put the sausages in a medium-size saucepan and add cold water to cover them. Over medium-high heat, bring the water to a boil. Drain the sausages immediately and prick each one in several places with the tines of a fork.

4. Brush the onion slices on both sides with olive oil and season lightly with salt and white pepper.

5. Grill or broil the sausage and onions until they are evenly browned, 4 to 5 minutes per side.

6. While the sausage and onions are cooking, put the arugula and radicchio leaves in a bowl and toss them with about two thirds of the dressing. Arrange the leaves in beds on large individual serving plates.

7. With a small, sharp knife, quarter the pears lengthwise and cut out their cores and stems. Cut each quarter lengthwise into thin slices and arrange them atop half of each salad.

8. With a fork, separate the onion rings and strew them on top of the salad halves not covered by the pears. Cut each sausage diagonally into ½-inch slices and arrange them on top of the onion rings. Scatter the raspberries all over each salad and garnish with the pine nuts and shredded basil. Serve immediately.

TEST KITCHEN NOTES

HERE'S A FINE EXAMPLE OF HOW A RICH AND SATISFYING MAIN INGREDIENT CAN BE TRANSFORMED INTO A LIGHT SALAD. THE SECRET, IN THIS CASE, LIES IN SELECTING ACCOMPANYING INGREDIENTS—IN THIS CASE, FRESH FRUIT AND A BERRY-SCENTED DRESSING—THAT OFFER SHARP, BRIGHT CONTRAST TO ITS RICHNESS, YIELDING AN OVERALL REFRESHING EFFECT THAT ALLOWS ONE TO LEAVE THE TABLE FEELING SATISFIED BUT NOT STUFFED.

FOR AN EXTRA-SPECIAL OCCASION, TRY MAKING IT WITH BONELESS DUCK BREASTS, USING ONE BREAST PER SERVING. YOU MAY HAVE TO SPECIAL-ORDER THEM FROM YOUR BUTCHER. MAKE A LITTLE EXTRA RASPBERRY VINAIGRETTE, PUT IT IN A SEPARATE BOWL, AND MARINATE THE DUCK BREASTS IN IT FOR ABOUT 30 MINUTES. THEN SEASON WITH SALT AND PEPPER AND GRILL OR BROIL UNTIL THEY ARE DONE TO YOUR LIKING; FOR MEDIUM-RARE, 3 TO 4 MINUTES PER SIDE.

Shaved Fennel Salad with Prosciutto and Parmesan

SERVES 4

DRESSING

¼ cup lemon juice
½ teaspoon salt
½ teaspoon sugar
¼ teaspoon white pepper
¾ cup extra-virgin olive oil

SALAD

4 fennel bulbs (about 3 pounds total)
6 ounces prosciutto, very thinly sliced
¼ pound (or more) block
    Parmesan cheese
¼ cup finely shredded fresh basil leaves

1. To make the dressing, stir together in a small bowl the lemon juice, salt, sugar, and pepper until the salt and sugar dissolve. Stirring continuously, slowly pour in the olive oil. Set the dressing aside.

2. With a sharp knife, trim off the stalk stumps and the root ends of the fennel bulbs. Cut each bulb in half, top to bottom. Place each half cut side down and cut it crosswise as thinly as possible to make thin strips. Put the fennel strips in a mixing bowl and toss with enough of the dressing to coat well.

3. Arrange the fennel salad in beds on large, chilled, individual serving plates. Drape the prosciutto slices on top of the fennel. Hold the block of Parmesan over each salad and, with a cheese shaver or a swivel-blade vegetable peeler, cut the cheese in wide, thin shavings, letting them fall on top of the prosciutto and using about ½ ounce of cheese per salad. Garnish each serving with the shredded basil.

TEST KITCHEN NOTES

THIS SALAD REMINDS ME OF A SUNNY AFTERNOON ON A *TERRAZZO* IN ITALY. IT IS INSPIRED, IN FACT, BY THE KIND OF FENNEL SALAD YOU MIGHT WELL FIND ON AN ITALIAN ANTIPASTO TABLE: THIN STRIPS OF THE CRISP, LICORICE-SCENTED BULB DRESSED WITH A SIMPLE LEMON VINAIGRETTE AND TOPPED WITH PARMESAN SHAVINGS. IN THIS CASE, IT WAS MY OWN IDEA TO ADD PROSCIUTTO, PARMA'S FAMED CURED RAW HAM, WHICH YOU CAN FIND IN ANY WELL-STOCKED ITALIAN DELICATESSEN OR SPECIALTY MARKET. NO DOUBT, THOUGH, YOU'D FIND SUCH A CREATION SOMEWHERE ON A TOUR OF TUSCANY.

BEFITTING THE SPIRIT OF THE SALAD, I SUGGEST SERVING IT AS A WARM-WEATHER LUNCH, ACCOMPANIED SIMPLY BY A CRUSTY LOAF OF GOOD, PEASANT-STYLE BREAD, SOME SOFTENED UNSALTED BUTTER FOR SPREADING, AND A CRISP, COOL ITALIAN WHITE WINE SUCH AS A VERDICCHIO OR PINOT GRIGIO.

Prosciutto and Minted Melon Salad

SERVES 4

1 honeydew melon
1 cantaloupe
¼ cup lemon juice
¼ cup honey
3 tablespoons finely chopped fresh
    mint leaves
4 cups mixed baby salad leaves
6 ounces prosciutto, very thinly sliced
3 ounces feta cheese, crumbled
    (optional)
Fresh mint sprigs, for garnish

1. Halve and seed the melons. If you like, use a melon ball scoop to remove the flesh in neat balls, transferring them to a mixing bowl. Alternatively, peel the rind from each melon half and cut the flesh into slices or neat chunks approximately 1 inch across.

2. Drizzle the lemon juice and honey over the melon pieces and toss well to coat them. Sprinkle on the chopped mint and toss again. If not serving the salad immediately, cover the bowl with plastic wrap and refrigerate for up to several hours.

3. Divide the melon pieces equally among four large, shallow, chilled serving bowls. Neatly drape the slices of prosciutto on top of the melon. Then arrange the baby salad leaves in beds next to the prosciutto. Garnish with crumbled feta cheese, if you like. Garnish each serving with a mint sprig.

TEST KITCHEN NOTES

ON A HOT SUMMER'S DAY, WHEN YOU WANT TO SERVE A LIGHT BUT REALLY FLAVORFUL AND SATISFYING MAIN-COURSE LUNCHEON SALAD, THIS MIGHT JUST DO THE TRICK. IT WAS INSPIRED BY THE CLASSIC ITALIAN APPETIZER OF PROSCIUTTO AND MELON, WHICH I HAVE LONG LOVED.

I FIND THIS SALAD A WINNER ON SEVERAL COUNTS. IT LOOKS BEAUTIFUL, THE MELONS' JEWELLIKE COLORS FORMING A BACKGROUND FOR THE DEEP, SLIGHTLY TRANSLUCENT ROSE HUE OF THE THINLY SLICED PROSCIUTTO. THE SALAD ALSO HAS A MELLOW, SALTY RICH TASTE AND CONTRASTING TEXTURES: THE SENSUOUS TEXTURE OF THE CURED ITALIAN HAM IS OFFSET BY THE BRIGHT, SWEET SPICINESS AND COOL JUICINESS OF THE MELON. FINALLY, YOU MIGHT APPRECIATE, AS I DO, THE WAY THIS SALAD ALLOWS YOU TO ENJOY JUST A LITTLE BIT OF FLAVORFUL RED MEAT WHILE MAINTAINING A SENSIBLY HEALTHY, RELATIVELY LOW-FAT DIET.

TO TURN THIS SALAD INTO A FIRST-CLASS MEAL, SERVE IT WITH A GLASS OF COOL, CRISP WHITE WINE THAT HAS AN EDGE OF FRUITINESS TO IT. BETTER STILL, ALLOW YOURSELF THE INDULGENCE OF A SPARKLING WINE—MAYBE ITALY'S ASTI SPUMANTE. FOR A TRULY OUTRAGEOUS EFFECT, INSTEAD OF CRISP ITALIAN BREAD, ACCOMPANY THE SALADS WITH PLAIN, CRISP ALMOND BISCOTTI.

Cold Steak and Rotelle Pasta Salad with Cherry Tomatoes

SERVES 4

DRESSING

1 cup Ranch Dressing (see page 26)

SALAD

¾ pound dried rotelle pasta

2 dozen cherry tomatoes, stemmed and
    cut in half

½ teaspoon salt

1 pound cooked beef steak, cooled and
    cut into thin, bite-size pieces

½ small red onion, thinly sliced

3 ounces arugula leaves, stemmed

6 cups mixed baby salad greens

2 tablespoons coarsely chopped
    Italian parsley

1. Prepare the dressing and set it aside.

2. Bring a large saucepan of water to a boil over medium-high heat. Add the rotelle and cook until firm-tender but still chewy, about 8 minutes or according to the package directions.

3. Drain the pasta in a strainer and rinse under cold running water until the pasta is cool. Drain well.

4. In a small mixing bowl, toss together the cherry tomato halves and the salt.

5. Put the pasta in a mixing bowl and add the tomatoes, steak, onion, and arugula. Toss gently to mix. Add the dressing and toss again until all the ingredients are evenly coated.

6. Arrange the baby salad leaves in beds on large, chilled, individual serving plates or bowls. Mound the salad on top and garnish with parsley.

TEST KITCHEN NOTES

THIS IS A GREAT RECIPE TO USE WHEN YOU'VE GRILLED OR BROILED A LARGE STEAK THE NIGHT BEFORE AND HAVE SOME LEFT OVER. IT ALSO WORKS JUST FINE WITH LEFT-OVER ROAST BEEF. IF YOU WANT TO COOK SOME STEAK ESPECIALLY FOR IT, JUST RUB THE MEAT WITH A LITTLE OLIVE OIL AND SPRINKLE GENEROUSLY WITH SALT AND PEPPER, THEN COOK TO TASTE; BE SURE TO ALLOW TIME FOR THE MEAT TO COOL BEFORE ASSEMBLING THE SALAD.

NOTE THAT IN THE RECIPE INSTRUCTIONS I CALL FOR THE CHERRY TOMATOES TO BE LIGHTLY SALTED BEFORE YOU ADD THEM TO THE OTHER INGREDIENTS. IN THIS PARTICULAR CONTEXT, WITH THE TOMATOES SET AGAINST THE PASTA AND CREAMY DRESSING, I FOUND THIS PRELIMINARY SALTING PUT THEIR FLAVOR INTO SHARPER RELIEF. BUT IF YOU'RE TRYING TO CUT BACK ON SALT, YOU CAN OMIT THIS STEP.

THE ARUGULA LEAVES ADD A PLEASING DASH OF DARK GREEN COLOR AND A HINT OF BITTERNESS TO THE MIXTURE. IF ARUGULA IS UNAVAILABLE, SUBSTITUTE BABY SPINACH LEAVES.

IF YOU PREFER, YOU COULD USE CLASSIC BLUE CHEESE DRESSING (SEE PAGE 25) OR A SIMPLE VINAIGRETTE OF BALSAMIC VINEGAR, DIJON MUSTARD, AND OLIVE OIL IN PLACE OF THE RANCH.

Tropical Fruit Sunburst

SERVES 4

DRESSING

½ cup honey, at room temperature
¼ cup lime juice
½ teaspoon pure ground chili powder

SALAD

2 ripe pineapples, well chilled
2 ripe mangoes, well chilled
2 ripe papayas, well chilled
4 ripe bananas
Fresh mint sprigs, for garnish

1. To make the dressing, stir together the honey and lime juice in a small mixing bowl until blended. Stir in the chili powder and set aside.

2. To prepare the salad, first, peel the pineapples. With a large, sharp knife, cut off the top and bottom of a pineapple. Stand the pineapple upright and, slicing downward, peel away its skin in thick strips. With the tip of a small, sharp knife, cut out any remaining tough "eyes" from the fruit. With the pineapple still upright, cut downward to slice the fruit away from the thick, woody central core; discard the core. Cut the fruit into long spears.

3. With a small, sharp knife, peel the mangoes. Then cut the fruit away from the large, flat central stones in thick slices. Cut the slices into long strips. Set aside with the pineapple.

4. Halve, peel, and seed the papayas and cut them lengthwise into ½-inch-thick slices. Set them aside with the mango and pineapple.

5. Finally, peel the bananas and cut them lengthwise into halves or thirds.

6. Arrange the fruit in starburst patterns on large, chilled, individual serving plates. With a spoon, drizzle the dressing evenly all over the fruit. Garnish with mint sprigs and serve immediately.

TEST KITCHEN NOTES

NOTHING CAN QUITE PREPARE YOU FOR HOW STARTLINGLY GOOD THIS SALAD TASTES. THE SECRET LIES IN THE HINT OF PURE RED CHILI POWDER THAT SPICES UP THE HONEY AND LIME JUICE IN THE SALAD'S DRESSING. THAT MAY SEEM ODD, I KNOW. THE CONCEPT RAISED MY EYEBROWS WHEN MY FRIEND JOHN SEDLAR, THE PIONEER OF MODERN SOUTHWESTERN CUISINE, FIRST SERVED ME HIS CHOCOLATE CHILI ICE CREAM. I WAS DELIGHTED, THOUGH, BY THE WAY THE WHISPER OF CHILI DEEPENED THE CHOCOLATE'S RICH FLAVOR AND THEN LEFT JUST A SUSPICION OF AFTERBURN ON THE PALATE.

THE CHILI SERVES A SIMILAR ROLE HERE. YOU MIGHT NOT EVEN KNOW IT IS THERE ON FIRST TASTE, THOUGH YOU WILL SEE BRICK RED SPECKS DOTTING THE FRUIT. ALL YOU'LL SENSE IS THAT THE FRUIT TASTES SOMEHOW SWEETER, THE CITRUSY HONEY MORE EXOTIC. THEN, JUST AS THE COOL FLAVORS HAVE PASSED, YOU'LL WONDER WHY YOU FEEL A LITTLE BIT OF HEAT IN YOUR MOUTH. AND JUST AS, SAY, THE SALT OF PEANUTS MAKES YOU WANT TO DRINK MORE BEER OR COLA, SO TOO DOES THE WARMTH OF THE CHILI SEND YOU BACK FOR ANOTHER TASTE OF THE FRUIT. IN SHORT, IT'S THE PERFECT LUNCHEON SALAD FOR A SULTRY DAY.

Summer Fruit Platter with Fresh Berry Yogurt

SERVES 4

FRESH BERRY YOGURT DIP

1 pound very ripe fresh berries

3 tablespoons honey

Grated zest of 1 lemon

3 cups plain yogurt

SALAD

1 small cantaloupe

4 plums

2 peaches

2 nectarines

1 pound cherries, whole with stems or
    pitted and sliced

Fresh mint sprigs, for garnish

1. For the dip, first sort through the berries, removing any stems and reserving several attractive ones for garnishing. Put the remaining berries in a mixing bowl and, using a potato masher or a fork, begin to mash them up. As soon as some of their juices show, drizzle in the honey and sprinkle in the lemon zest. Continue mashing until the berries are coarsely puréed, with some small lumps still showing. Stir in the yogurt until well blended, then cover with plastic wrap and refrigerate.

2. Shortly before serving time, prepare the fruit. Cut the melon into thin wedges, scoop out the seeds, and, with a sharp knife, carefully cut away the peel. Halve and pit the plums, peaches, and nectarines, and cut them into wedges.

3. Divide the yogurt among four small bowls, each one in the center of a large, chilled serving plate. Arrange the fruit wedges around the bowl and intersperse the cherries, their stems on. Garnish the yogurt with the reserved whole berries and sprigs of mint. Alternatively, arrange all the fruit on the chilled plates, garnish with mint, and serve the yogurt on the side as a dressing. Serve immediately.

TEST KITCHEN NOTES

THE BEST ADVICE I CAN GIVE YOU ON THIS SALAD IS THAT IT SHOULD BE DIFFERENT EVERY SINGLE TIME YOU MAKE IT, REFLECTING THE EVER-CHANGING ARRAY OF WONDERFUL SUMMER FRUITS AVAILABLE IN THE BEST LOCAL GREENGROCER, FARMERS' MARKET, OR SUPERMARKET YOU CAN FIND.

MELONS ARE A MUST, WHETHER CANTALOUPE OR HONEYDEW OR ANY OF THE OTHER LUSCIOUS BUT MORE FLEETING VARIETIES. (WATERMELON, HOWEVER, IS A LESS LIKELY CANDIDATE BECAUSE IT DOESN'T REALLY GO AS WELL WITH THE YOGURT DIP.) BUT THE REAL STARS OF THIS SALAD SHOULD BE JUICY SUMMER STONE FRUIT. PEACHES, OF COURSE, AND PREFERABLY A FREESTONE VARIETY. NECTARINES, NATURALLY. PLUMS CAN ADD GREAT VARIETY; I'M ESPECIALLY PARTIAL TO THE DEEP GARNET-COLORED BLACKFRIAR TYPE, AS WELL AS TO SPECKLED REDDISH-ORANGE DAPPLE DANDY PLUMS. CHERRIES ADD A FINAL, FESTIVE NOTE, WHETHER THE MOST COMMON RED BING OR, MY FAVORITES, THE BLUSHING YELLOW-RED RAINIER OR QUEEN ANNE.

$Sources$

Throughout this book, I have tried to use ingredients that are widely available. When I call for ingredients that might be the least bit specialized, I discuss in the recipe's Test Kitchen Notes where you can find them or what you can use in their place.

However, if you cannot find particular ingredients, or if you simply like to seek out new products through the mail, I offer the following list of sources for salad-related products, including not only ingredients but also cookware. Write, phone, or fax for further information.

ASIAN SPECIALTIES

House of Spice–Kensington
  Market
190 Auguste Street
Toronto, ON
M5T 2L6
phone: (416) 593-9724

Katagiri
224 East 59th Street
New York, NY 10022
phone: (212) 752-4197

S. Eakin, Inc.
1203 St. Lawrence
Montreal, PQ
H2X 2S6

BREADS

Bread Alone, Inc.
Route 28
Boiceville, NY 12412
phone: (914) 657-3328
fax: (914) 657-6228

Dimpflmeier Bakery
26 Advance Road
Toronto, ON
M87 2TA
phone: (416) 239-3031

Empire Baking Company
4264 Oaklawn Avenue
Dallas, TX 75219
phone: (214) 526-3223
fax: (214) 526-3394

Tree Mouse Edibles Inc.
RR4, Site 430, C-32
Courtenay, BC V9N 7J3
Canada
phone: (905) 945-5090
fax: (905) 945-1128
fine selection of German breads

Gazin's
P.O. Box 19221
New Orleans, LA 70119
phone: (504) 482-0302
New Orleans-style French bread

CHEESES

Brier Run Farm
HC 32, Box 73
Birch River, WV 26610
phone: (304) 649-2975
fresh goat cheese

Fitz-Henri Fine Foods
1875 Leslie Street, Unit 14
Willowdale, ON
M2K 1E6
phone: (416) 225-4175
*imported cheeses, jams, and
  other fine foods*

Ideal Cheese Shop
1205 Second Avenue
New York, NY 10021
phone: (800) 382-0109
          (212) 688-7579

Mt. Capra Cheese
279 S.W. 9th Street
Chehalis, WA 98532
phone: (206) 748-4224
fresh goat cheese

Maytag Dairy Farms
P.O. Box 806
Newton, IA 50208
phone: (800) 247-2458
fax: (515) 792-1567
blue cheese

Mozzarella Company
2944 Elm Street
Dallas, TX 75226
phone: (800) 798-2954
          (214) 741-4072
fax: (214) 741-4076
*fresh mozzarella and goat
  cheese*

Rogue River Valley Creamery
311 N. Front
Central Point, OR 97505
phone: (503) 664-2233
blue cheese

Sadie Kendall Cheese
P.O. Box 686
Atascadero, CA 93423
phone: (805) 466-7252
fresh goat cheese

COOKWARE AND DISHES

Dean & Deluca
560 Broadway
New York, NY 10012
phone: (800) 221-7714
          (212) 226-6800
fax: (800) 781-4050

Saffron's
Manotick Mews Shopping
  Center
Box #208
Manotick, ON
K4M 1A3
phone: (613) 692-2064
fine foods and kitchenware

Williams-Sonoma
P.O. Box 7456
San Francisco, CA 94120
phone: (800) 541-2233
fax: (415) 421-5153

Worldwide Imported
  Foods, Inc.
6700 Cote des Neiges
Montreal, PQ
H3S 2B2
phone: (514) 948-5603
*international gourmet foods
  and cookware*

NUTS AND DRIED FRUITS

The Girdled Grape Raisin Co.
P.O. Box 345
Sultana, CA 93666
phone: (209) 626-4094
fax: (209) 626-4902
raisins

Hazy Grove Nuts
P.O. Box 25753
Portland, OR 97201
phone: (800) 574-6887
          (503) 244-0593
hazelnuts

Mac Farms of Hawaii
3615 Harding Street,
  Suite 207
Honolulu, HI 96816
phone: (800) 737-0645
fax: (808) 734-4675
Macadamia nuts

Nunes Farms
P.O. Box 311
Newman, CA 95360
phone: (800) 255-1641
        (209) 862-3033
fax: (209) 862-1038
almonds

Sable & Rosenfeld
15 Elm Street
Toronto, ON
M5T 2X7
phone: (416) 929-4214

San Saba Pecan, Inc.
2803 West Wallace
San Saba, TX 76877
phone: (800) 621-8121
        (915) 372-5727
fax: (915) 327-5729
pecans

Timber Crest Farms
4791 Dry Creek Road
Healdsburg, CA 95448
phone: (707) 433-8251
fax: (707) 433-8255

OILS, VINEGARS, AND CONDIMENTS

Firefly Foods Company
P.O. Box 82096
Portland, OR 97282
phone: (800) 745-6215
fax: (503) 659-2650
herb-flavored vinegars

Island Kitchens
Stuart Island, BC V0P 1V0
Canada
phone (250)287-6370
fax: (250) 287-0018
flavored vinegars

Fusana California Valley
  Specialty Olive Company
P.O. Box 11576
Piedmont, CA 94611
phone: (800) 916-5483
        (510) 530-3516
fax: (510) 531-1083
olive oils and cured olives

Napa Valley Kitchens
1236 Spring Street
St. Helena, CA 94574
phone: (800) 288-1089
        (707) 967-1107
fax: (707) 967-1117
mustards and flavored olive oils

Kendall-Brown Foods
86 Forrest Lane
San Rafael, CA 94903
phone: (800) 851-7203
        (415) 499-1621
fax: (415) 472-5737
raspberry vinegar

Nick Sciabica & Sons
P.O. Box 1246
Modesto, CA 95353
phone: (800) 551-9612
        (209) 577-5067
fax: (209) 524-5367
olive oils

Pasquale Brothers
  Downtown, Ltd.
217 King Street East
Toronto, ON
M58 1JA
phone: (416) 364-7397
retail gourmet groceries

Santa Barbara Olive
  Company
P.O. Box 1570
Santa Ynez, CA 93460
phone: (800) 624-4896
        (805) 688-9917
fax: (805) 686-1659
olive oils and cured olives

SAUSAGES

AE Price Fine Foods, Ltd.
130 Esplanade Laurier
Ottawa, ON K2P 1W5
phone: (613) 232-3557
fresh meat, produce, herbs

Aidells Sausage Company
1575 Minnesota Street
San Francisco, CA 94107
phone: (800) 541-2233
fax: (415) 421-5153

The Galloping Goose
  Sausage Company
4484 Lindholm Road
Metchosina, BC V9C 3Y1
Canada
phone: (250) 474-5788
low-fat, high-quality sausages

Gerhard's Napa Valley
  Sausage
901 Enterprise Way
Napa, CA 94558
phone: (707) 252-4116
fax: (707) 252-0879

SEAFOOD

Clearwater Fine Foods Inc.
757 Bedford Highway
Bedford, NS B4A 3Z7
Canada
phone: (902) 443-0550
fax: (902) 443-8365
freesh lobster and seafood

Lazio Family Products
327 Second Street
Eureka, CA 95501
phone: (800) 737-6688
        (707) 442-6688
fax: (707) 442-5867

Legal Seafoods Market
5 Cambridge Center
Main at 6th
Cambridge, MA 02139
phone: (800) 343-5804
        (617) 864-3400
fax: (617) 254-5809
fresh fish and shellfish

Royalty Seafood
  Enterprises, Inc.
25 Carle Road, Suite 102
Westbury, NY 11590
phone: (888) 522-3474
fax: (516) 334-5052
fresh fish and shellfish

S.T. Moore Seafood
27510 Ocean Gateway
Hebron, MD 21830
phone: (800) 325-2722
fax: (410) 546-1681
*fresh Maryland crabmeat and
  other seafood*

VEGETABLES AND SALAD LEAVES

American Spoon Foods
P.O. Box 566
Petoskey, MI 49770
phone: (800) 222-5886
fax: (800) 647-2512
mushrooms

Aux Delices des Bois
14 Leonard Street
New York, NY 10013
phone: (212) 334-1230
fax: (212) 334-1231
mushrooms

Balducci's
424 Avenue of the Americas
New York, NY 10011
phone: (800) 225-3822
fax: (718) 786-4125

Bland Farms
P.O. Box 506, Route 4
Highway 169
Glennville, GA 30427
phone: (800) 843-2542
fax: (912) 654-4280
sweet Vidalia onions

Diamond Organics
P.O. Box 2159
Freedom, CA 95019
phone: (800) 922-2396
        (408) 763-1993
fax: (408) 763-2444
organic salad leaves and other
* produce*

Frieda's Rare & Exotic Foods
P.O. Box 58488
Los Angeles, CA 90058
phone: (800) 241-1771
        (714) 826-6100
fax: (714) 816-0277

Hickins Mountain Mowings
  Farm and Greenhouse
RFD 1, Black Mountain
  Road, Box 293
Brattleboro, VT 05301
phone: (802) 254-2146
salad leaves, baby vegetables,
* and other produce*

COMMON METRIC CONVERSIONS

DRY MEASURES (BY WEIGHT)		LIQUID MEASURES (BY VOLUME)	
IMPERIAL	METRIC	IMPERIAL	METRIC
2 oz.	60g	1 tsp.	5ml
2.5 oz.	75g	1 tbsp.	15ml
3 oz.	90g	2 tbsp.	30ml
3.5 oz.	105g	4 tbsp.	60ml
4 oz.	125g	3 fl oz.	90ml
5 oz.	150g	4 fl oz.	125ml
6 oz.	175g	5 fl oz.	150ml
7 oz.	215g	6 fl oz.	175ml
8 oz.	250g	7 fl oz.	200ml
10 oz.	300g	8 fl oz. (1 cup)	250ml
12 oz.	375g	10 fl oz.	300ml
16 oz. (1 lb)	500g	12 fl oz.	375ml

Index